Reflections from Psalm 119

by Kenneth O. Light

DORRANCE
PUBLISHING CO
EST. 1920
PITTSBURGH, PENNSYLVANIA 15238

Dorrance Publishing Co
585 Alpha Drive
Pittsburgh, PA 15238
Visit our website at *www.dorrancebookstore.com*

ISBN: 979-8-88925-415-7
eISBN: 979-8-88925-915-2

Reflections
from Psalm 119

FOREWORD

I have read Psalm 119 many times, but the Holy Ghost has heightened my interest in the content in my latter years upon this earth. This Psalm offers encouragement, correction, direction, happiness, comfort, definition of and reasoning for things that happen in life.

The Psalmist broke Psalm 119 into 22 alphabetical Hebrew units to not only help the reader to learn and understand the Hebrew alphabet, but to be happy and successful in serving God, King David was not only a man after the heart of God; he was a prolific writer. His writings were full of wisdom which taught those who read the words that flowed from his spirit to learn and practice many successful things in the 21st century as we are led by the Holy Ghost into the depth of the meaning of his ancient words!

We are not to be just religious. We are to be born again by the Spirit Christians filled and baptized with the Holy Ghost in order to have power, become victorious and prosperous in our Father's vineyard as we lay up treasure in Heaven for ourselves though good works. John 15 and Ephesians 2: 10

Faithfulness [Titus 3:8] is a must to accomplish our portion of the harvest field he has called us too, but sometimes it is hard to get under our bodies and bring them into subjection [1 Corinthians 9:27], but we can and will accomplish that if we do it joyfully .

The word of God is laid out in a library of 66 books which contain all the knowledge we need; nuggets of gold which are priceless. These books teach absolute truth and focus upon God's everlasting love [Jeremiah 31:3] for us and how we can obtain and capture happiness through obedience to his predestinated will [Romans 8:29] for each of us to be more than conquerors in our life time [Romans 8:37]. It is our choice to conform to the image of his son; we are not forced!

Our Father in Heaven, our Creator, desires for us to be happy and fulfilled in the days of our pilgrimage here on earth, then he gives us assurance of an eternal existence where there are no more challenges in our life because we chose to become born again by the Spirit. John 3:1-7

Through this study, let us allow the Holy Ghost to lead us into all blessedness as we learn and accept God's desire for our lives which is to find happiness and peace no matter what happens in our lives while we are pilgrims and strangers on this earth. 1 Peter 2:11

It is my prayer this study will be one that is laced with the mercy and grace of God instead of a job description for us to follow. We must worship and serve our Father in spirit and truth. John 4:24.

This study will probably be incomplete as the scriptures are of no private interpretation. [2 Timothy 3:16; 2 Peter 1:19-21] I urge each person who chooses to read this study to go deeper in the Word.

I view the holy scriptures as a personal love letter from our Father in order for each of us to walk and do his bidding in a willing and faithful manner because we love him. I do not consider myself a slave, but a child of God growing under the influence of his grace and mercy as I extend it the same to others.

<u>Note:</u> all scripture references are from the authorized King James Version of the Holy Bible; various commentaries found in the PC Study Bible Version 5 and personal experiences over 50 plus years of ministry.

UNIT ONE:

ALWPH
Psalm 119: 1-8

<u>VERSE ONE:</u> *"Blessed are the undefiled in the way; who walk in the law of the Lord."*

<u>THE FIRST THING MENTIONED IS WE MUST BE UNDEFILED:</u> The only way mankind can be viewed as undefiled is as those who are born again by the Spirit, baptized in water and cleansed by the Blood of the Lamb.

"There was a man of the Pharisees, named Nicodemus, a ruler of the Jews: The same came to Jesus by night, and said unto him, Rabbi, we know that thou art a teacher come from God: for no man can do these miracles that thou doest, except God be with him. Jesus answered and said unto him, Verily, verily, I say unto thee, Except a man be born again, he cannot see the kingdom of God. Nicodemus saith unto him, How can a man be born when he is old? Can he enter the second time into his mother's womb, and be born? Jesus answered, Verily, verily, I say unto thee, except a man be born of water and of the Spirit, he cannot enter into the kingdom of God. That which is born of the flesh is flesh; and that which is born of the Spirit is spirit. Marvel not that I said unto thee, ye must be born again." John 3:1-7

"Wherefore, holy brethren, partakers of the heavenly calling, consider the Apostle and High Priest of our profession, Christ Jesus; who was faithful to him that appointed him, as also Moses was faithful in all his house. For this man was counted worthy of more glory than Moses, inasmuch as he who hath builded the house hath more honour than the house. For every house is builded by some man; but he that built all things is God. And Moses verily was faithful in all his house, as a servant, for a testimony of those things which were to be spoken after; But Christ as a son over his own house; whose house are we, if we hold fast the confidence and the rejoicing of the hope firm unto the end. Wherefore (as the Holy Ghost saith, today if ye will hear his voice, Harden not your hearts, as in the provocation, in the day of temptation in the wilderness: When your fathers tempted me, proved me, and saw my works forty years. Wherefore I was grieved with that generation, and said, they do alway err in their heart; and they have not known my ways. So I sware in my wrath, they shall not enter into my rest. Take heed, brethren, lest there be in any of you an evil heart of unbelief, in departing from the living God. But exhort one another daily, while it is called Today; lest any of you be hardened through the deceitfulness of sin. For we are made partakers of Christ, if we hold the beginning of our confidence steadfast unto the end; While it is said, today if ye will hear his voice, harden not your hearts, as in the provocation. For some, when they had heard, did provoke: howbeit not all that came out of Egypt by Moses. But with whom was he grieved forty years? Was it not with them that had sinned, whose carcasses fell in the wilderness? And to whom sware he that they should not enter into his rest, but to them that believed not? So we see that they could not enter in because of unbelief." Hebrews 3: 1-19

"And one of the elders answered, saying unto me, What are these which are arrayed in white robes? And whence came they? And I said unto him, Sir, thou knowest. And he said to me, These are they which came out of great tribulation, and have washed their robes, and made them white in the blood of the Lamb. Therefore are they before the throne of God, and serve him day and night in his temple: and he that sitteth on the throne shall dwell among them. They shall hunger no more, neither thirst anymore; neither shall the sun light on them, nor any heat. For the Lamb which is in the midst of the throne shall feed them, and shall lead them unto

living fountains of waters: and God shall wipe away all tears from their eyes." Revelation 7: 13-17

THE SECOND THING SPOKEN: WE MUST BE OBEDIENT:

Webster defines the word *obedience* as: submission, complying to commands and directions and Holy Ghost anointed power. Our reaction to God must be as a ship obeys her helm which is controlled by the Captain.

We as born again by the Spirit believers are the Bride of Christ; we are to love and obey our soon coming Groom Jesus the Christ because he is absolute authority! He is the great *I AM* who gave himself as a sacrifice in order for us to have the privilege of being saved from our self-centered sinful life and life-styles for all eternity. We are ships upon the sea of life, but Jesus is the Captain of our helm.

"…he that endureth to the end shall be saved." Matthew 10: 22

"Thou therefore endure hardness, as a good soldier of Jesus Christ. No man that warreth entangleth himself with the affairs of this life; that he may please him who hath chosen him to be a soldier. And if a man also strive for masteries, yet is he not crowned, except he strive lawfully. The husbandman that laboureth must be first partaker of the fruits." 2 Timothy 2: 3-6

Jesus prayed the Father [John 14: 16, 17] to send us the Holy Ghost to comfort, empower, and guide us into all truth. God did not send us this great gift of anointing for us to become prideful and take our God-given liberty to the occasion of the flesh [Galatians 5: 13]. Neither did he send the Holy Ghost for us to create man-made doctrines; he sent us the Holy Ghost anointing to empower us to preach and teach the full gospel of Jesus Christ that flows from Genesis 1 through Revelation 22: 21 without inserting our fleshly prideful display of human analyzation and doctrine. The Apostle Paul stated in 2 Timothy 2: 15:

"Study to shew thyself approved unto God, a workman that needeth not to be ashamed, rightly dividing the word of truth."

VERSE TWO: *"Blessed are they that keep his testimonies, and that seek him with the whole heart."*

Psalm 9: 7-11, 2 Timothy 3: 16, 17 and Matthew 22: 37-40 provide the order of our individual testimonies as individual members of the body of Christ. Our individual talents are to consummate one purpose. That is to believe, exalt and obey our Fathers Son: John 6: 29.

> *"The law of the LORD is perfect, converting the soul: the testimony of the LORD is sure, making wise the simple. The statutes of the LORD are right, rejoicing the heart: the commandment of the LORD is pure, enlightening the eyes. The fear of the LORD is clean, enduring forever: the judgments of the LORD are true and righteous altogether. More to be desired are they than gold, yea, than much fine gold: sweeter also than honey and the honeycomb. Moreover by them is thy servant warned: and in keeping of them there is great reward." Psalm 19: 7-11*

> *"All scripture is given by inspiration of God, and is profitable for doctrine, for reproof, for correction, for instruction in righteousness: That the man of God may be perfect, throughly furnished unto all good works." 2 Timothy 3: 16, 17*

> *"Thou shalt love the Lord thy God with all thy heart, and with all thy soul, and with all thy mind. This is the first and great commandment. And the second is like unto it, Thou shalt love thy neighbour as thyself. On these two commandments hang all the law and the prophets." Matthew 22: 37-40*

> <u>*VERSE THREE:*</u> *"They also do no iniquity: they walk in his ways."*

The word *iniquity* used in this verse comes from the Hebrew word meaning *distorted morality*. Unfortunately, many professing confessing Christians in our 21st century churches are walking in *distorted morality* and will wind up in hell unless they repent. Romans 1: 18-32

Because of Jesus Chris's shed blood, resurrection and assentation, we have the privilege to receive him into our hearts and become born again by the Spirit. This being the case, we are to not walk in the way of iniquity; we are to walk in his ways just as he did while he was here on earth for approximately 33½ years.

When we face temptations and trials, we have a helper called the Holy Ghost who will guard our thought life, if we will let him. Jesus left us these words in John 14: 15-18 and 26, 27 which are for you and me in the 21st century.

> *"If ye love me, keep my commandments. And I will pray the Father, and he shall give you another Comforter, that he may abide with you forever; Even the Spirit of truth; whom the world cannot receive, because it seeth him not, neither knoweth him: but ye know him; for he dwelleth with you, and shall be in you. I will not leave you comfortless: I will come to you. But the Comforter, which is the Holy Ghost, whom the Father will send in my name, he shall teach you all things, and bring all things to your remembrance, whatsoever I have said unto you. Peace I leave with you, my peace I give unto you: not as the world giveth, give I unto you. Let not your heart be troubled, neither let it be afraid."*

When he ascended to Heaven, he became our High Priest. Hebrews 4: 14-16; 5: 1-10. He knows the pressures of life; he lived as a human being for 33½ years. He understands human nature and can help us become overcomers through the power of the Holy Ghost.

> *"Wherefore in all things it behoved him to be made like unto his brethren, that he might be a merciful and faithful high priest in things pertaining to God, to make reconciliation for the sins of the people. For in that he himself hath suffered being tempted, he is able to succour them that are tempted." Hebrews 2: 17, 18*

The word *succour* comes from three Greek words meaning help and relieve. So when you feel that you cannot make it on your own, you have help. Listen to the following verse:

> *"Humble yourselves therefore under the mighty hand of God, that he may exalt you in due time: Casting all your care upon him; for he careth for you." 1 Peter 5: 6, 7*

> <u>*VERSE FOUR:*</u> *"Thou commanded us to keep thy precepts diligently."*

When God gave Moses the commandments and Moses related the law to the Israelites, they were to obey the law to the letter; if they did not, they suffered the consequences. It did not take long for them to start living the way they wanted to and adding amendments to the law to justify their sinful lifestyles. Deuteronomy 32: 10-31

Jesus preached the Sermon on the Mount to the Israelites informing them how to live a blessed life in Matthew 5: 1-48. The Israelites rejected his teaching and wound up crucifying him.

The question comes to my mind: *"Why do we human beings refuse the good and accept the bad when things are clearly explained to them?"* That is a question that needs to be considered by all confessing professing Christians who are playing church instead of worshiping God in spirit and in truth. The truth is: the professing confessing Christians need to become born again by the Spirit!

As we consider verse 4 of psalm 119, let us remember the following challenge:

> *"Behold, I set before you this day a blessing and a curse; A blessing, if ye obey the commandments of the LORD your God, which I command you this day: And a curse, if ye will not obey the commandments of the LORD your God, but turn aside out of the way which I command you this day, to go after other gods, which ye have not known." Deuteronomy 11: 26-28*

> *"I call heaven and earth to record this day against you, that I have set before you life and death, blessing and cursing: therefore choose life, that both thou and thy seed may live: That thou mayest love the LORD thy God, and that thou mayest obey his voice, and that thou mayest cleave unto him: for he is thy life, and the length of thy days: that thou mayest dwell in the land which the LORD sware unto thy fathers, to Abraham, to Isaac, and to Jacob, to give them." Deuteronomy 30: 19, 20*

One might say, those verses are ancient and do not apply to the modern day Christian because we live in the day of grace. May I say, the word of God is current and relevant from Genesis 1:1 through Revelation 22: 21. Why? Because God is omnipotent, omnipresent and omniscient; he is not confined by time as we are. Plus, he states: *"I am the Lord, I change not"* Malachi 3: 6.

Jesus states in Matthew 5: 17, 18:

> *"Think not that I am come to destroy the law, or the prophets: I am not come to destroy, but to fulfil. For verily I say unto you, till heaven and earth pass, one jot or one tittle shall in no wise pass from the law, till all be fulfilled."*

> *"Therefore we conclude that a man is justified by faith without the deeds of the law. Is he the God of the Jews only? is he not also of the Gentiles? Yes, of the Gentiles also: Seeing it is one God, which shall justify the circumcision by faith, and uncircumcision through faith. Do we then make void the law through faith? God forbid: yea, we establish the law." Romans 3:28-31*

Webster defines the word *'diligently"* as constant action.

> *VERSE FIVE AND SIX:* *"O that my ways were directed to keep thy statues! Then I shall not be ashamed, when I have respect unto all thy commandments."*

The word *statues* used in this verse comes from the Hebrew word that means *"appointed ordinance"*.

Many people confuse the word *predestination* and some determine that they will go to Heaven by just walking by God's appointed ordinance, which is just keeping the Ten Commandments. As stated earlier in this study, Jesus clearly stated the *"ye must be born again by the spirit,"* John 3: 1-7.

We must come clean within ourselves and consider the words of Jesus concerning our heavenly citizenship.

Jesus was blessing the children one day, and when he had finished, he was approached by a man that everyone would consider and good Christian man.

> *"And when he was gone forth into the way, there came one running, and kneeled to him, and asked him, Good Master, what shall I do that I may inherit eternal life? And Jesus said unto him, Why callest thou me good? there is none good but one, that is, God. Thou knowest the commandments, Do not commit adultery, Do not kill, Do not steal, Do not bear false witness, Defraud not, Honour thy father and mother. And he answered and said unto him, Master,*

If you will compare the commandments that he had observed, you will note that he had only obeyed part of the ten. He was a good man, but not totally sold out to God. He went away without being born again by the Spirit because of self-centeredness and greed.

David was a man after God's own heart, yet he was not perfect! He was however a seeker of God's presence; God will honor mankind by hearing their repentant prayers and praise. Then he will guide them into truth by the Holy Ghost.

thee, the freewill offerings of my mouth, O LORD, and teach me thy judgments. My soul is continually in my hand: yet do I not forget thy law." Psalm 119: 97-109

Let us continually cry out: *"O that my ways were directed to keep thy statues!"*

VERSE SEVEN AND EIGHT: "I will praise thee with uprightness of heart, when I shall have learned thy righteousness judgments. I will keep the statues: O forsake me not utterly."

I have learned through personal experience that humble praise of our Father's greatness and thanking him for his existence in the universe is a great way to initiate sweet fellowship. He is not an arrogant God that needs our praise and appreciation, but he knows humankind needs to build a relationship in order to become fulfilled in our daily walk here on Earth.

Keeping his word active in our spirit and communication with each other ensures His presence in our life as we travel our path here on earth.

"As he spake by the mouth of his holy prophets, which have been since the world began: That we should be saved from our enemies, and from the hand of all that hate us; To perform the mercy promised to our fathers, and to remember his holy covenant; The oath which he sware to our father Abraham, That he would grant unto us, that we being delivered out of the hand of our enemies might serve him without fear, In holiness and righteousness before him, all the days of our life." Luke 1: 70-75

Luke was a physician, and he knew a healthy relationship with God promoted good physical and spiritual health.

I love psalm 33; it speaks volumes concerning the reason for praising God for his care and righteous judgments:

"Rejoice in the LORD, O ye righteous: for praise is comely for the upright. Praise the LORD with harp: sing unto him with the psaltery and an instrument of ten strings. Sing unto him a new song; play skillfully with a loud noise. For the word of the LORD is right; and all his works are done in truth. He loveth righteousness and judgment: the earth is full of the goodness of the LORD. By the

word of the LORD were the heavens made; and all the host of them by the breath of his mouth. He gathereth the waters of the sea together as an heap: he layeth up the depth in storehouses. Let all the earth fear the LORD: let all the inhabitants of the world stand in awe of him. For he spake, and it was done; he commanded, and it stood fast. The LORD bringeth the counsel of the heathen to nought: he maketh the devices of the people of none effect. The counsel of the LORD standeth forever, the thoughts of his heart to all generations. Blessed is the nation whose God is the LORD: and the people whom he hath chosen for his own inheritance. The LORD looketh from heaven; he beholdeth all the sons of men. From the place of his habitation he looketh upon all the inhabitants of the earth. He fashioneth their hearts alike; he considereth all their works. There is no king saved by the multitude of an host: a mighty man is not delivered by much strength. An horse is a vain thing for safety: neither shall he deliver any by his great strength. Behold, the eye of the LORD is upon them that fear him, upon them that hope in his mercy; to deliver their soul from death, and to keep them alive in famine. Our soul waiteth for the LORD: he is our help and our shield; for our heart shall rejoice in him, because we have trusted in his holy name. Let thy mercy, O LORD, be upon us, according as we hope in thee." Psalm 33: 1-22

UNIT TWO:

BETH
Psalm 119: 9-16

<u>VERSE NINE:</u> "Wherewithal shall a young man cleanse his way? By taking heed thereto according to thy word."

I have often wished I had begun studying the word of God at a much younger age. I read the word as a teenager, but I did not take the time to get acquainted with the author through prayer and study.

When I was born again by the Spirit at the age of 26, I only studied the portions I liked and that not very well; I thought they were easily understood. In short I was a very shallow Christian for several years. But there came a day in prayer when the Holy Ghost spoke to my heart and told me if I intended to preach and teach the word of God, I needed the Holy Ghost to lead me into deeper truth and understanding. From that time, I began yielding to the leadership of the Holy Ghost and have learned many things, and I am still learning at the age of 81!

"The proverbs of Solomon the son of David, king of Israel; To know wisdom and instruction; to perceive the words of understanding; To receive the instruction of wisdom, justice, and judgment, and equity; To give subtilty to the simple, to the young man knowledge and discretion. A wise man will hear, and will increase learning; and a man of understanding shall attain unto wise counsels: To understand

a proverb, and the interpretation; the words of the wise, and their dark sayings. The fear of the LORD is the beginning of knowledge: but fools despise wisdom and instruction." Proverbs 1: 1-7

"My son, if thou wilt receive my words, and hide my commandments with thee; So that thou incline thine ear unto wisdom, and apply thine heart to understanding; Yea, if thou criest after knowledge, and liftest up thy voice for understanding; If thou seekest her as silver, and searchest for her as for hid treasures; Then shalt thou understand the fear of the LORD, and find the knowledge of God. For the LORD giveth wisdom: out of his mouth cometh knowledge and understanding. He layeth up sound wisdom for the righteous: he is a buckler to them that walk uprightly. He keepeth the paths of judgment, and preserveth the way of his saints. Then shalt thou understand right-eousness, and judgment, and equity; yea, every good path." Proverbs 2: 1-9

I remember a fellow missionary making a statement to me one time when I was struggling with some scriptures; he said: *"Brother, there comes a time when you have to get desperate and cry out to God for understanding through the Holy Ghost."* He was right and when I began to do that, the Holy Ghost began to open my understanding. That was Brother Paul Evans who is now in Heaven with Jesus.

"Get wisdom, get understanding: forget it not; neither decline from the words of my mouth. Forsake her not, and she shall preserve thee: love her, and she shall keep thee. Wisdom is the principal thing; therefore get wisdom: and <u>with all thy getting get understanding</u>. Exalt her, and she shall promote thee: she shall bring thee to honour, when thou dost embrace her. She shall give to thine head an ornament of grace: a crown of glory shall she deliver to thee." Proverbs 4: 5-9

<u>*VERSE TEN*</u>: *"With my whole heart have I sought thee: O let me not wander from thy commandments."*

I have stated many times to young ministers and born again by the Spirit Christians, God only requires 10% of our money, but he demands 100% of our time, mind, heart and soul to be in loving obedience to his Word.

David made a lot of mistakes and committed adultery and had a man killed, but he was a man after God's own heart. Why? His tenacity and love for God was without fault.

> *"Praise ye the LORD. I will praise the LORD with my whole heart, in the assembly of the upright, and in the congregation. The works of the LORD are great, sought out of all them that have pleasure therein. His work is honourable and glorious: and his righteousness endureth forever. He hath made his wonderful works to be remember-ed: the LORD is gracious and full of compassion. He hath given meat unto them that fear him: he will ever be mindful of his covenant. He hath shewed his people the power of his works, that he may give them the heritage of the heathen. The works of his hands are verity and judgment; all his commandments are sure. They stand fast for ever and ever, and are done in truth and uprightness. He sent redemption unto his people: he hath commanded his covenant for ever: holy and reverend is his name. The fear of the LORD is the beginning of wisdom: a good understanding have all they that do his commandments: his praise endureth forever." Psalm 111: 1-10*

My prayer as I write this study is whoever reads it will receive the quickening of the Holy Ghost and become strong in the Lord's work!

> *<u>VERSE ELEVEN</u>: "Thy word have I hid in mine heart, that I might not sin against thee."*

Born again by the Spirit Christians must not presume upon God's grace and mercy. Also we who are pastors, evangelist, missionaries, Sunday school teachers, and deacons must not presume that we are exempt of presumption because of our office and ministry.

Peter, in his second letter, dealt very strongly concerning our spiritual conduct.

> *"The Lord knoweth how to deliver the godly out of temptations, and to reserve the unjust unto the day of judgment to be punished: But chiefly them that walk after the flesh in the lust of uncleanness, and despise government. Presumptuous are they, selfwilled, they*

are not afraid to speak evil of dignities. Whereas angels, which are greater in power and might bring not railing accusation against them before the Lord. But these, as natural brute beasts, made to be taken and destroyed, speak evil of the things that they understand not; and shall utterly perish in their own corruption; And shall receive the reward of unrighteousness, as they that count it pleasure to riot in the day time. Spots they are and blemishes, sporting themselves with their own deceiving while they feast with you; Having eyes full of adultery, and that cannot cease from sin; beguiling unstable souls: an heart they have exercised with covetous practices; cursed children: Which have forsaken the right way, and are gone astray, following the way of Balaam the son of Bosor, who loved the wages of unrighteous-ness; But was rebuked for his iniquity: the dumb ass speaking with man's voice forbad the madness of the prophet. These are wells without water, clouds that are carried with a tempest; to whom the mist of darkness is reserved for ever. For when they speak great swelling words of vanity, they allure through the lusts of the flesh, through much wantonness, those that were clean escaped from them who live in error. While they promise them liberty, they themselves are the servants of corruption: for of whom a man is overcome, of the same is he brought in bondage. For if after they have escaped the pollutions of the world through the knowledge of the Lord and Saviour Jesus Christ, they are again entangled therein, and overcome, the latter end is worse with them than the beginning. For it had been better for them not to have known the way of righteousness, than, after they have known it, to turn from the holy commandment delivered unto them. But it is happened unto them according to the true proverb, The dog is turned to his own vomit again; and the sow that was washed to her wallowing in the mire." 2 Peter 2: 9-22

As I read these scriptures and thought upon them, I cried out to God as David did in Psalm 19: 7-14

"The law of the LORD is perfect, converting the soul: the testimony of the LORD is sure, making wise the simple. The statutes of the LORD are right, rejoicing the heart: the commandment of the LORD is pure, enlightening the eyes. The fear of the LORD is clean, enduring for ever: the judgments of the LORD are true and righteous altogether. More to be desired are they than gold, yea,

than much fine gold: sweeter also than honey and the honeycomb. Moreover by them is thy servant warned: and in keeping of them there is great reward. Who can understand his errors? Cleanse thou me from secret faults. <u>Keep back thy servant also from presumptuous sins; let them not have dominion over me: then shall I be upright, and I shall be innocent from the great transgression. Let the words of my mouth, and the meditation of my heart, be acceptable in thy sight, O LORD, my strength, and my redeemer.</u>"

When we presumptuously sin, we fall under the category of the word *"sinneth"*. This word indicates the continuance of a sinful lifestyle, not as single sin that we may commit in the process of our day. Even so, we must work the works of repentance as a born again by the Spirit Christian. Acts 26: 19, 20; I John 1: 6-10

"The soul that sinneth, it shall die. The son shall not bear the iniquity of the father, neither shall the father bear the iniquity of the son: the righteousness of the righteous shall be upon him, and the wickedness of the wicked shall be upon him." Ezekiel 18: 20

Lord, help me to become contentious of my lifestyle and walk in the light as you are in the light.

<u>VERSE TWELVE:</u> "Blessed art thou, O Lord teach me thy statutes."

The word *statutes* comes from the Hebrew word *chog* which means *commandment, custom, decree, ordinance or task.* In the Old Testament, people were dependent on the prophets to teach them the things of God; in the New Testament, we must become humble before God and allow ourselves to be taught by the leadership of the Holy Ghost.

I fear we in the 21st century church we have forgotten many of the customs of our worship of God; we have become critical of music styles, dress codes, etc. that we have forgotten why we come into the Sanctuary! We are not to compare ourselves nor lower our standards. But we must conform to the image of our lord Jesus Christ. Romans 8: 29.

In many Pentecostal churches, I have found that there is more emphasis placed on the speaking of tongues than on the teaching of why the tongues were used on the day of the outpouring of the Holy Ghost. In one of the churches I pastored, there were those who professed they were more holy than others because they spoke in tongues in every service. Don't get me wrong, I believe wholly in the ministry of the gifts of the Spirit, but shall we not demonstrate the fruit of the Spirit and allow the Holy Ghost anointing to flow at God's directive instead of human perspective? I challenged myself to study the happening on the day of Pentecost to really understand the purpose of speaking in tongues. The church of Corinth wandered off into sin and miss-representation of this wonderful gift and the apostle Paul dealt with them in a strong but loving manner finally stating the following:

"Yet in the church I had rather speak five words with my understanding, that by my voice I might teach others also, than ten thousand words in an unknown tongue. Brethren, be not children in
understanding: howbeit in malice be ye children, but in understanding be men." 1 Corinthians 14: 19, 20

Let us learn the scriptures and then allow the truth to flow from us through the precious anointing of the Holy Ghost which will bring God the glory of all that transpires in our personal life and worshiping God!

"Blessed art thou, O Lord teach me thy statutes."

<u>VERSES THIRTEEN AND FOURTEEN:</u> "With my lips have
I declared all the judgments of thy mouth. I have rejoiced in the
way of thy testimonies, as much as in all riches."

We must know our in own heart the danger of sinful lifestyles; God is long-suffering in mercy but we must fear and tremble in repentance or suffer the consequences. We must be happy to be found in the path of obedience, giving our whole heart and strength to God, and when enabled to do it, we should rejoice more in it than monetary gain. We must realize how great the treasure of a tender and approving conscience before our God!

> *"A good man out of the good treasure of his heart bringeth forth that which is good; and an evil man out of the evil treasure of his heart bringeth forth that which is evil: for of the abundance of the heart his mouth speaketh." Luke 6: 45*

> *VERSES FIFTEEN AND SIXTEEN: "I will meditate in thy precepts; and have respect unto thy ways. I will delight myself in thy statutes: I will not forget thy word."*

When we read and think on the victories of God's people as they faithfully obeyed his word in the Old Testament then think on the ministry of Jesus in the New Testament, we become encouraged by the Holy Ghost to continue the fight of faith and be more than conquerors.

In my personal times of worship and prayer, sometimes I get so excited that I become emotionally charged because of what God has done and will do in me *if* I will obey his word to the letter. I have been known to run around in my office and in the sanctuary because of the joy the Holy Ghost has given me.

Turn to Psalm chapter 18: 1-50; read and meditate on David's time of victory! I believe after you have read a few verses you will be shouting the victory in your life for all God has done for you. When the Lord had delivered David from the hand of all his enemies and from the hand of Saul, he had a great time rejoicing and proclaiming God's goodness! I guarantee, when you get through that chapter, you'll find yourself shouting praises to God in the highest and forget about all the problems you may be facing. Try it, it works!

UNIT THREE:
GIMEL
Psalm 119: 17-24

VERSE SEVENTEEN: _"Deal bountifully with servant, that I may live, and keep thy word."_

This is my cry to my God in these latter days. I do not need anything or any money; he has supplied for my wife and myself in a bountiful way in our declining years on this Earth. But what I do need is more of God's holy anointing and open doors to do his work until he takes me home.

PROVERB 22: 9 STATES: _"He that hath a bountiful eye shall be blessed; for he giveth of his bread to the poor."_

The question arises as I read this verse: _Who are the poor?_

JESUS STATED IN THE BEATITUDES: _"Blessed are the poor in spirit: for theirs is the kingdom of heaven." Matthew 5: 3_

ISAIAH PROPHESIED THE FOLLOWING IN CHAPTER 57 VERSE 15-21:

"For thus saith the high and lofty One that inhabiteth eternity, whose name is Holy; I dwell in the high and holy place, with him *also that is of a contrite and humble spirit, to revive the spirit of the humble, and to revive the heart of the contrite ones. For I will not contend for ever, neither will I be always wroth: for the spirit should fail before me, and the souls which I have made. For the iniquity of his covetousness was I wroth, and smote him: I hid me, and was wroth, and he went on forwardly in the way of his heart. I have seen his ways, and will heal him: I will lead him also, and restore com-forts unto him and to his mourners. I create the fruit of the lips; Peace, peace to him that is far off, and to him that is near, saith the LORD; and I will heal him. But the wicked are like the troubled sea, when it cannot rest, whose waters cast up mire and dirt. There is no peace, saith my God, to the wicked."*

NOTE OF CLARITY:

We as born again by the Spirit Christians are not to neglect being charitable to those who are less fortunate. We are to give to the poor with the intent to help them become able to find help for themselves morally and spiritually; unfortunately, for the last fifty years or more, there are people who have become totally dependent upon charity instead of trying to help themselves out of the problem they are in. We need to give them a *hand up* instead of a *hand out* to help them restore their dignity and responsibility. Of course there are exceptions; some people are mentally and physically not able to do this, so it is our duty to help them.

When Jesus was approached by the rich young man with the following question, , *"Good Master, what good thing shall I do, that I may have eternal life?"* (Matthew 19: 16), Jesus knew his heart; he was a fine young man who evidently led a good moral life from his youth. But he only obeyed part of the commandments. He had the means of purchasing anything he desired. He desired eternal life, but he found out he could not purchase it without giving his all. He had to make a choice! Unfortunately he chose not to obey the words of Christ because he worshipped his standing in the community of the rich!

"Jesus said unto him, If thou wilt be perfect go and sell that thou hast, and give to the poor, and thou shalt have treasure in heaven: and come and follow me." Matthew 19: 21

Being a born again by the Spirit Christian is not about money; it is about commitment! On the other hand, being flat broke does not qualify one as a Christian. I have a few friends who are very well off financially, some are millionaires and they are faithful Christians who are very liberal in giving way above their tithe. Then there those who give all as the woman in Mark 12: 41-44:

"…Jesus sat over against the treasury, and beheld how the people cast money into the treasury: and many that were rich cast in much. And there came a certain poor widow, and she threw in two mites, which make a farthing. And he called unto him his disciples, and saith unto them, Verily I say unto you, that this poor widow hath cast more in, than all they which have cast into the treasury: For all they did cast in of their abundance; but she of her want did cast in all that she had, even all her living."

JESUS SUMS IT UP EVERYTHING IN MATTHEW 6: 33:

"…seek ye first the kingdom of God, and his righteousness; and all these things shall be added unto you."

This simply means God is our source of material things and eternal salvation through Jesus Christ our Lord.

VERSE EIGHTEEN: "Open thou mine eyes, that I may behold wondrous things out of thy law."

There is an old hymn written and set to music by Clara H. Scott in 1895 entitled "Open my eyes that I may see"; read the following lyrics and maybe sing to your spirit the following words:

"Open my eyes that I may see glimpses of truth thou hast for me; place in my hands the wonderful key that shall unclasp and set me free; silently now I wait for thee, ready, my God, thy will to see; open my eyes illumine me Spirit divine!

Open my ears that I may hear voices of truth thou sendest clear; and while the wave-notes fall on my ear, ev-'ry-thing false will dis-

appear: silently now I wait for thee, ready, my God, thy will to see; open my ears illumine me Spirit divine!

Open my mouth and let me bear gladly the warm truth ev-'ry-where; open my heart, and let me prepare love with thy children thus to share: silently now I wait for thee, ready, my God, thy will to see; open my heart illumine me Spirit divine!"

What an unselfish prayer! Sometimes we Christians are so self-centered in our prayer life; it all has to be for me and my family. There are a lot of people around us each day who would love to hear good news. My prayer to this fact is: *help me find them* then be sensitive to the still small voice of God in order to minister to them properly!

"The secret of the LORD is with them that fear him; and he will shew them his covenant. Mine eyes are ever toward the LORD; for he shall pluck my feet out of the net." Psalm 25: 14-15

"The eyes of the LORD are upon the righteous, and his ears are open unto their cry." Psalm 34: 15

THE WONDEROUS THING CONCERNING GOD IS FOUND IN JOHN 3: 16-21!

"For God so loved the world that he gave his only begotten Son, that whosoever believeth in him should not perish, but have ever-lasting life. For God sent not his Son into the world to condemn the world; but that the world through him might be saved. He that believeth on him is not condemned: but he that believeth not is condemned already, because he hath not believed in the name of the only begotten Son of God. And this is the condemnation, that light is come into the world, and men loved darkness rather than light, because their deeds were evil. For every one that doeth evil hateth the light, neither cometh to the light, lest his deeds should be reproved. But he that doeth truth cometh to the light that his deeds may be made manifest, that they are wrought in God."

Let us be full of God's everlasting love for those who are created in his image and lead them to the truth by walking in the righteousness of Jesus not our own.

> *VERSES NINETEEN AND TWENTY: "I am a stranger in the earth: hide not thy commandments from me. My soul breaketh for the longing that it hath unto thy judgments at all times."*

Sometimes God lets us feel like we're walking alone, but be it known, he is omnipresent! He is everywhere with everybody he has created. He is watching and waiting for us to hunger and thirst after his righteousness. He never will forsake a broken heart and a contrite spirit. I feel him in the wind, in the rain; I hear him in the thunder and his still small voice in the quietness of the night. He is ever near me! Selah!

However, to really know him we must seek his face in honest confession of our sins and ask for his forgiveness in the name of his precious son. The measure of faith that is given to each person when they are born is quickened by the Holy Ghost who moves in our spirit when we realize that we no longer can control our life; each of us know we need help. Many of us go to the wrong places that bring us the feeling of security through unrighteous lifestyles. But that security never proves it self to be true.

As I am writing this study, I am going into my 79th year; my journey on this Earth has not been perfect, but my Jesus is. He presents me faultless before my Father as I walk in the light as he is in the light.

> *"Now unto him that is able to keep you from falling, and to present you faultless before the presence of glory with exceeding joy. To the only wise God our Saviour be glory and majesty, dominion and power, both now and ever. Amen." Jude verses 24, 25*

> *"Praise ye the Lord: for it is good to sing praises unto or God; for it is pleasant; and praise is comely." Psalm 147: 1*

> *VERSES TWENTY-ONE THROUGH TWENTY-FOUR: "Thou hast rebuked the proud that are cursed, which do err from thy commandments. Remove from me reproach and contempt; for I have kept thy testimonies. Princes also did sit and speak against me: but thy servant did meditate in thy statutes. Thy testimonies also are my delight and my counsellors."*

> *"I will therefore put you in remembrance, though ye once knew this, how that the Lord, having saved the people out of the land of Egypt, afterward destroyed them that believed not. And the angels which kept not their first estate, but left their own habitation, he hath reserved in everlasting chains under darkness unto the judgment of the great day. Even as Sodom and Gomorrah, and the cities about them in like manner, giving themselves over to fornication, and going after strange flesh, are set forth for an example, suffering the vengeance of eternal fire likewise also these filthy dreamers defile the flesh, despise dominion and speak evil of dignities. Yet Michael the archangel, when contending with the devil he disputed about the body of Moses, durst not bring against him a railing accusation, but said, The Lord rebuke thee. But these speak evil of those things which they know not: but what they know naturally, as brute beasts, in those things they corrupt themselves. Woe unto them! for they have gone in the way of Cain, and ran greedily after the error of Balaam for reward, and perished in the gainsaying of Core."*

We as born again by the Spirit believers can cast out devils, but Jesus our Lord is the only one who has the divine authority to rebuke Satan!

> *"Then certain of the vagabond Jews, exorcists, took upon them to call over them which had evil spirits the name of the Lord Jesus, saying, We adjure you by Jesus whom Paul preacheth. And there were seven sons of one Sceva, a Jew, and chief of the priests, which did so. And the evil spirit answered and said, Jesus I know, and Paul I know; but who are ye? And the man in whom the evil spirit was leaped on them, and overcame them, and prevailed against them, so that they fled out of that house naked and wounded. And this was known to all the Jews and Greeks also dwelling at Ephesus; and fear fell on them all, and the name of the Lord Jesus was magnified."*

In the Scripture above, the seven sons of Sceva were already practicing exorcisms, and they took on themselves to try to do what Paul preached and failed; the man who was possessed prevailed against them. Why? Because they

were doing it with secondhand knowledge of the work of the Spirit; they had
no spiritual authority.

We are to gain spiritual authority to do two major things in order for us
to live victoriously on earth! 1. To live a faithful fulfilling life. 2. To become
empowered by the Holy Ghost to carry out the great commission!

THE APOSTLE PAUL TELLS HOW IN 2 TIMOTHY 2: 15, 16:

*"Study to shew thyself approved unto God, a workman that needeth
not to be ashamed, rightly dividing the word of truth. But shun
profane and vain babblings: for they will increase unto more ungodliness."*

UNIT FOUR:

DALETH
Psalm 119: 25-32

VERSE TWENTY-FIVE: _"My soul cleaveth unto dust: quicken thou me according to thy word."_

The dictionary describes the word _cleaveth_ with two definitions:

1. To stick; to adhere; to be attached; to cling: used both in the literal and figurative sense.
2. To unite or be united closely in interest or affection; to adhere with strong attachment; to be faithful.

When we become born again by the Spirit, the very first thing we must do is ask the Holy Ghost to help us love his Word so much that we hunger and thirst after a more deeper truth.

The following is only my conviction; I believe a person who really has an experience will do just that. Many go to their own denominational seminary to analyze and study the history of the Bible and to learn a lot of how to preach and pastor. That is not all wrong. However, many of our seminaries are being infiltrated with men and women teachers who are agnostic and do not really believe that the word of God is relevant in the 21st century!

I was very blessed to have several mentors who helped and encouraged me through my early years of Christian life. Plus, because I could not afford to go to Bible College, I took assigned courses through the Berean School of the Bible by correspondence and received my certificate of ordination from the Assemblies of God denomination. But I received most of my practical Biblical knowledge from my mentors, intense study and by the leadership of the Holy Ghost.

Through the Holy Ghost baptism, I received the quickening of my spirit to receive what I was studying. Carnal analyzation of the Word profits little!

> *"There is therefore now no condemnation to them which are in Christ Jesus, who walk not after the flesh, but after the Spirit. For the law of the Spirit of life in Christ Jesus hath made me free from the law of sin and death. For what the law could not do, in that it was weak through the flesh, God sending his own Son in the likeness of sinful flesh, and for sin, condemned sin in the flesh: That the righteousness of the law might be fulfilled in us, who walk not after the flesh, but after the Spirit; For they that are after the flesh do mind the things of the flesh; but they that are after the Spirit the things of the Spirit. For to be carnally minded is death; but to be spiritually minded is life and peace. Because the carnal mind is enmity against God: for it is not subject to the law of God, neither indeed can be. So then they that are in the flesh cannot please God. But ye are not in the flesh, but in the Spirit, if so be that the Spirit of God dwell in you. Now if any man have not the Spirit of Christ, he is none of his. And if Christ be in you, the body is dead because of sin; but the Spirit is life because of righteousness. But if the Spirit of him that raised up Jesus from the dead dwell in you, he that raised up Christ from the dead shall also quicken your mortal bodies by his Spirit that dwelleth in you." Romans 8: 1-11*

Kneeolgy can do far more for a person studying the Word than theological teaching!

VERSE TWENTY-SIX: *"I have declared my ways, and thou heardest me: teach me thy statues."*

As I read this verse, I became amused at myself because I have done just that! In my past, I have rehearsed my cares, troubles, anxieties, and complaints to God many times. God allowed me to stew in my situation, and I did not hear or feel his presence in my life for a few days. When I came to myself, I felt like the prodigal son in the hog pen. So I began to repent and cry out to God in humble contrition, and guess what? He heard my prayer and answered it!

The Holy Ghost came upon me a few years ago, and I began to love the Word more than I had ever loved it before. I feared and trembled before him and began to work on my attitude.

It is only when we declare all our ways before God properly that we can hope he *will* respond to our prayer. It is right and proper that we should go before God with all our cares and troubles. There is nothing that gives us anxiety of which we may not speak to him; however trivial as it may seem to be as a child speaks to a parent of the smallest matter that troubles him or her. When this is done, we may be assured that God will not turn away from us or disregard our cry. He loves us through our problems when we express our love and trust in him!

> *"Humble yourselves therefore under the mighty hand of God, that he may exalt you in due time: Casting all your care upon him; for he careth for you. Be sober, be vigilant; because your adversary the devil, as a roaring lion, walketh about, seeking whom he may devour: Whom resist stedfast in the faith, knowing that the same afflictions are accomplished in your brethren that are in the world. But the God of all grace, who hath called us unto his eternal glory by Christ Jesus, after that ye have suffered a while, make you perfect, stablish, strengthen, settle you. To him be glory and dominion for ever and ever. Amen." 1 Peter 5: 6-11*

<u>VERSE TWENTY-SEVEN</u>: *"Make me to understand the way of thy precepts: so shall I talk of thy wondrous works."*

When I was a kid, no one could make me do anything without physical force which was usually a whipping. But they could entice me to participate if I knew there was a reward. You might say I was a bullish, self-centered, red-haired, freckle-faced kid.

We as born again by the Spirit Christians are sometimes like that because we do not understand the reward of God's precepts. That is why Jesus prayed the Father to send us the Holy Ghost to comfort us and lead us into all Truth. The Holy Ghost will move upon our heart and call upon him to *"melt us, mold us, fill us, and use us"*. When we get to that position in our spirit, God will pour himself into our thinking process through the Holy Ghost, and before we know it, we will begin to spread the good news of God and enjoy doing it.

> *"But ye, beloved, building up yourselves on your most holy faith, praying in the Holy Ghost, Keep yourselves in the love of God, looking for the mercy of our Lord Jesus Christ unto eternal life. And of some have compassion, making a difference: And others save with fear, pulling them out of the fire; hating even the garment spotted by the flesh. Now unto him that is able to keep you from falling, and to present you faultless before the presence of his glory with exceeding joy, To the only wise God our Saviour, be glory and majesty, dominion and power, both now and ever. Amen." Jude 20-25*

> <u>*VERSE TWENTY-EIGHT*</u>: *"My soul melteth for heaviness: strengthen thou me according unto thy word."*

Sometimes in our time here on Earth as pilgrims and strangers, we are wearied with sudden discouragements. The continual problem after problem begins to weaken our faith and we fail to renew our strength.

When this happens, we must depend upon the Comforter to help by leading us to scriptures of encouragement.

When I give into to this type of discouragement, I turn to my favorite scriptures:

> *"Hast thou not known? hast thou not heard, that the everlasting God, the LORD, the Creator of the ends of the earth, fainteth not, neither is weary? There is no searching of his understanding. He giveth power to the faint; and to them that have no might he increaseth strength. Even the youths shall faint and be weary, and the young men shall utterly fall: But they that wait upon the LORD shall renew their strength; they shall mount up with wings as eagles; they shall run, and not be weary; and they shall walk, and not faint." Isaiah 40: 28-31*

"Fear thou not: for I am with thee: be not dismayed: for I am thy God: I will strengthen thee; yea, I will help thee; yea, I will uphold thee with right hand of my righteousness. For I the Lord thy God will hold thy right hand, saying unto thee, Fear not; I will help thee." Isaiah 41: 10, 13

<u>VERSES TWENTY-NINE THROUGH THIRTY-TWO</u>: *"Remove from me the way of lying: and grant me thy law graciously. I have chosen the way of truth: thy judgments have I laid before me. I have stuck unto thy testimonies: O Lord, put me not to shame. I will run the way of thy commandments, when thou shalt enlarge my heart."*

I am ashamed to confess that sometimes I have exaggerated the truth which is a form of lying. It is not only lying; it is a form of boasting which leads to pride. In my opinion, pride is the most dangerous of the basic three sins. Why? Because pride deals with the spiritual part of our being instead of the physical part of our being! Pride begins as a subtle deceitful satisfaction of our actions instead of thanking God for his work we are doing with the talents and abilities He has given us!

The truth sets a person free, but deceit puts one in bondage, and at the end of the journey is hell.

"He that overcometh shall inherit all things; and I will be his God, and he shall be my son. But the fearful, and unbelieving, and the abominable, and murderers, and whoremongers, and sorcerers, and idolaters, and all liars, shall have their part in the lake which burneth with fire and brimstone: which is the second death." Revelation 21: 7-8

My personal prayer concerning the sin of lying and my conversation in general is the verse found in Psalm 141: 3. *"Set a watch, O Lord, before my mouth; keep the door of my lips."*

Among all the ministries I have been involved with, I am very happy to be the age I am and doing what I can for God. His statues are always on my mind, and they guide my conduct as I serve him in truth and humility.

I have chosen to cleave to Biblical truth and travel the narrow path and am seeking the straight gate in which I soon will enter because of his grace and mercy.

By the help of the Holy Ghost, I will not let myself be disappointed or confounded; I am enjoying the fellowship I have with my heavenly Father though the leadership of the Holy Ghost and the friendship of my Lord Jesus Christ as I obediently walk in the light as he is in the light. Jesus is my scepter of righteousness!

I will not merely keep his commandments; I am determined to walk in them and keep them. As long as God gives me the energy, I will continue to proclaim them to whosoever will listen.

I ask God to acknowledge my dependence to express my understanding of what it means to be free from hindrances to what is right and share it with whomever will listen. I find the hearts of many are filled with selfishness, pride, vanity, ambition, and covetousness. I recognize those things because I have been there myself, and still have to guard myself from them. Sin has captured many by religion, instead of Biblical Christianity.

MAN MADE RELIGIONS WILL CAUSE FEAR INSTEAD OF PEACE WHICH WILL LEAD TO WHAT LUKE STATES IN CHAPTER 21 VERSES 26-28:

> *"Men's hearts failing them for fear, and for looking after those things which are coming on the earth: for the powers of heaven shall be shaken. And then shall they see the Son of man coming in a cloud with power and great glory. And when these things begin to come to pass, then look up, and lift up your heads; for your redemption draweth nigh."*

UNIT FIVE:

HE
Psalm 119: 33-40

VERSE THIRTY-THREE: _"Teach me, O LORD, the way of thy statutes; and I shall keep it unto the end."_

The word _teach_ used in this verse is from the Hebrew word meaning to properly throw, to cast, to hurl; and then, to teach as if truth were thrown and scattered abroad. This reminds me of the parable of the sower.

"Know ye not this parable? and how then will ye know all parables? The sower soweth the word. And these are they by the way side, where the word is sown; but when they have heard, Satan cometh immediately, and taketh away the word that was sown in their hearts. And these are they likewise which are sown on stony ground; who, when they have heard the word, immediately receive it with gladness; And have no root in themselves, and so endure but for a time: afterward, when affliction or persecution ariseth for the word's sake, immediately they are offended. And these are they which are sown among thorns; such as hear the word, And the cares of this world, and the deceitfulness of riches, and the lusts of other things entering in, choke the word, and it becometh unfruitful. And these are they which are sown on good ground; such as hear the word, and receive it, and bring forth fruit, some thirtyfold, some sixty, and some an hundred." Mark 4: 13-20

I believe we are responsible to spread the seed of the Word to everyone, but it is the responsibility of the individual to accept it. God is the one who draws man to himself, and God is the one who gives the increase. However, I believe if we will pray and seek God's face, he will give us a discernment of spirits and we will have the ability to know how to recognize good ground and begin to cultivate it properly before we seed it with the Word of God.

> _VERSE THIRTY-FOUR:_ _"Give me understanding, and I shall keep thy law; yea, I shall observe it with my whole heart."_

> _Proverbs 4: 7 states: "Wisdom is the principal thing; therefore get wisdom: and with all thy getting get understanding."_

There are many people who have wisdom concerning natural and physical processes, but they do not have the ability to think out how to achieve the full benefit of whatever they choose to do. Understanding is related to practical comprehension of a physical or spiritual achievement.

Example: I understand how to build a house, but I do not have the understanding of what materials I must use to bring it to completion. Sometimes we as born again by the Spirit Christians are somewhat the same; we know the mechanics of witnessing, but we do not know how help a person to really become a born again by the Spirit Christian.

I believe one must seek wisdom with an undivided mind and spirit in order to have the ability to gain understanding.

> _"If any of you lack wisdom, let him ask of God, that giveth to all men liberally, and upbraideth not; and it shall be given him. But let him ask in faith, nothing wavering. For he that wavereth is like a wave of the sea driven with the wind and tossed. For let not that man think that he shall receive any thing of the Lord. A double minded man is unstable in all his ways." James 1: 5-8_

> _VERSE THIRTY-FIVE:_ _"Make me to go in the path of thy commandments; for therein do I delight."_

Our Father will not force us to follow his commandments. That becomes very clear when you chart the pilgrimage of Israel in the wilderness. He created us with a free will to choose to love and obey him or not to do so.

If we will ask him, he will direct us in our way. To faithfully follow his will, we must depend upon his purpose for the direction he is leading us. This is called faith!

There is an interesting little word *haply* that denotes the following:

1. If therefore, if accordingly, if in these circumstances. Mark 11:13, of Christ and the fig tree.
2. If in consequence, Acts 17:27, if haply they might feel after God, in consequence of seeking him.
3. Lest ever, lest haply, Luke 14: 29, of laying a foundation, with the possibility of being unable to finish the building; Acts 5: 39, of the possibility of being found fighting against God; Hebrews 3: 2, lest haply, of the possibility of having an evil heart of unbelief. Lest at any time of testing, Matthew 4: 6; 5: 25; 13: 15; Mark 4:12; Luke 4:11; 21: 34; Hebrews 2:1; Matthew 25:9, 1 Timothy 2: 25..

As I read all the above, I have come to the conclusion that if I *haply* desire and have pleasure in God's commandments, I will have of a strong desire to keep them, and pray for grace that I may be able to do it.

VERSE THIRTY-SIX: "Incline my heart unto thy testimonies, and not to covetousness."

When I begin to study for a message to preach or teach, I ask the Holy Ghost to show me special words contained in the scripture I am led too that will touch the heart of those I am called to speak.

I realize if I depend upon my own spirit, I will not hit the mark intended: especially if I know the congregation and their problems.

There are more ministers turned away from preaching the correct messages by the sin of covetousness than any other sin. Pride is at the bottom of this sin. We are not to seek glory for a good sermon; we are to give glory to God because he has set his anointing upon us and spoke truth to his people.

"Let no man say when he is tempted, I am tempted of God: forGod cannot be tempted with evil, neither tempteth he any man: But every man is tempted, when he is drawn away of his own lust, and enticed." James 1: 13, 14

We as ministers of the gospel should fashion ourselves after the apostle Paul:

"For yourselves, brethren, know our entrance in unto you, that it was not in vain: But even after that we had suffered before, and were shamefully entreated, as ye know, at Philippi, we were bold in our God to speak unto you the gospel of God with much contention. For our exhortation was not of deceit, nor of uncleanness, nor in guile: But as we were allowed of God to be put in trust with the gospel, even so we speak; not as pleasing men, but God, which trieth our hearts. For neither at any time used we flattering words, as ye know, nor a cloke of covetousness; God is witness: Nor of men sought we glory, neither of you, nor yet of others, when we might have been burdensome, as the apostles of Christ. But we were gentle among you, even as a nurse cherisheth her children: So being affectionately desirous of you, we were willing to have imparted unto you, not the gospel of God only, but also our own souls, because ye were dear unto us." 1 Thessalonians 2:1-8

<u>*VERSE THIRTY-SEVEN:*</u> *"Turn away mine eyes from beholding vanity; and quicken thou me in thy way."*

We as born again by the Spirit Christians should be thankful in this world that we have eyelids; let us be careful what we take into our eyes because what we see is forever captured in our memory if we lust after it.

We must pray for the Holy Ghost to endow us with life, energy, vigor to enable us to walk in the way of holiness.

"He that walkedth righteously; and speaketh uprightly; he that despiseth the gain of oppressions, that shaketh his hands from holding of bribes, that stoppeth his ears from hearing of blood, and shutteth his eyes from seeing evil; He shall dwell on high: his place of defence shall be the munitions of rocks: bread shall be given him; his waters shall be sure." Isaiah 33:15

<u>VERSE THIRTY-EIGHT:</u> *"Stablish thy word unto thy servant, who is devoted to thy fear."*

In today's world, there is so much analyzing of the Word of God that it has caused a lot of vacillating from the truth of Scripture in the Christian world that skepticism is at a high level.

What should we preachers do about it?

In my opinion, when the Word of God says *"thus saith the Lord"* we must stand on the rock and preach the truth, not try to figure out why he made the statement. It is humans' place to accept and believe the Word that has endured the ages. Men have tried to destroy the Bible by fire, shredding, etc. but have not been successful; one day the "WORD" of God will be heard and seen as it is. Until then we must establish ourselves through the leading of the Holy Ghost and then preach the Word by faith.

John the revelator saw the following in Revelation 19: 11-16:

> *"And I saw heaven opened, and behold a white horse; and he that sat upon him was called Faithful and True, and in righteousness he doth judge and make war. His eyes were as a flame of fire, and on his head were many crowns; and he had a name written, that no man knew, but he himself. And he was clothed with a vesture dipped in blood: and his name is called The Word of God. And the armies which were in heaven followed him upon white horses, clothed in fine linen, white and clean. And out of his mouth goeth a sharp sword, that with it he should smite the nations: and he shall rule them with a rod of iron: and he treadeth the winepress of the fierceness and wrath of Almighty God. And he hath on his vesture and on his thigh a name written, KING OF KINGS, AND LORD OF LORDS."*

I am devoted to reverent fear of staying with what the Word of God states instead of what some theologians have conjured up. We can have the mind of Christ, but we cannot have the mind of God!

> *"For who hath known the mind of the Lord, that he may instruct him? But we have the mind of Christ."* 1 Corinthians 2:16; Philippians 2: 5

<u>*VERSE THIRTY-NINE:*</u> *"Turn away my reproach which I fear: for thy judgments are good."*

Preachers who choose to preach the truth that Jesus Christ is the Son of the living God, and no man can come to the Father but by him will always suffer reproach. I used to be upset by that, but I am not offended anymore because I love the Word of God more than worldly theology.

"Great peace, have they which love thy law: and nothing shall offend them." Psalm 119: 165

"Now I would not have you ignorant, brethren, that oftentimes I purposed to come unto you, (but was let hitherto,) that I might have some fruit among you also, even as among other Gentiles. I am debtor both to the Greeks, and to the Barbarians; both to the wise, and to the unwise. So, as much as in me is, I am ready to preach the gospel to you that are at Rome also. For I am not ashamed of the gospel of Christ: for it is the power of God unto salvation to every one that believeth; to the Jew first, and also to the Greek. For therein is the righteous-ness of God revealed from faith to faith: as it is written, The just shall live by faith. Romans 1: 13-17

<u>*VERSE FORTY:*</u> *"Behold, I have longed after thy precepts: quicken me in thy righteousness."*

If we want to become overcoming victorious Christians, we must long to know and experience the wonderful presence of God and appear before him in righteousness through Jesus the Christ. Then read and study his Word and allow the Holy Ghost to quicken our minds to the truth.

"Because the carnal mind is enmity against God: for it is not subject to the law of God, neither indeed can be. So then they that are in the flesh cannot please God. But ye are not in the flesh, but in the Spirit, if so be that the Spirit of God dwell in you. Now if any man have not the Spirit of Christ, he is none of his. And if Christ be in you, the body is dead because of sin; but the Spirit is life because of righteousness. But if the Spirit of him that raised up Jesus from the dead dwell in you, he that raised up Christ from the dead shall

also quicken your mortal bodies by his Spirit that dwelleth in you. Therefore, brethren, we are debtors, not to the flesh, to live after the flesh. For if ye live after the flesh, ye shall die: but if ye through the Spirit do mortify the deeds of the body, ye shall live. For as many as are led by the Spirit of God, they are the sons of God. For ye have not received the spirit of bondage again to fear; but ye have received the Spirit of adoption, whereby we cry, Abba, Father. The Spirit itself beareth witness with our spirit, that we are the children of God: And if children, then heirs; heirs of God, and joint-heirs with Christ; if so be that we suffer with him, that we may be also glorified together." Romans 8: 7-17

UNIT SIX:
VAU
Psalm 119: 41-48

__VERSE FORTY-ONE:__ "Let thy mercies come also unto me, O LORD, even thy salvation, according to thy word."

When we as born again by the Spirit Christians approach the throne of God, we should always realize that God is ready to extend his mercy because of our position in Christ Jesus. He desires to manifest his mercy upon his children. However, let us never presume upon his mercy. He is God; he already knows our heart and our motive.

We must always pray according to his will!

Jesus himself prayed for his father's will in the garden:

"Father, if thou be willing, remove this cup from me: nevertheless not my will, but thine, be done." Luke 22: 42

__VERSE FORTY-TWO:__ "So shall I have wherewith to answer him that reproacheth me: for I trust in thy word."

There are times in our lives that we may suffer a reproach and we don't know how to handle it. The first thing to do is not tell anyone or seek anyone's advice. I thank God every day for Jesus who is my advocate and counselor; we can trust his fidelity and know he keeps things in confidence. When we pray in his name, the Holy Ghost will direct us to the appropriate scriptures to deal with our feelings and give us wisdom to settle the problem that caused the reproach.

> *"And when thou prayest, thou shalt not be as the hypocrites are: for they love to pray standing in the synagogues and in the corners of the streets, that they may be seen of men. Verily I say unto you, they have their reward. But thou, when thou prayest, enter into thy closet, and when thou hast shut thy door, pray to thy Father which is in secret; and thy Father which seeth in secret shall reward thee openly. But when ye pray, use not vain repetitions, as the heathen do: for they think that they shall be heard for their much speaking. Be not ye therefor like them: for your Father knoweth what things ye have need of, before ye ask him." Matthew 6: 5-8*

> *VERSE FORTY-THREE:* *"And take not the word of truth utterly out of my mouth; for I have hoped in thy judgments."*

Many times when we come to God in prayer, our spirit is troubled and we do not know how to pray. It is at that time we must depend upon the Holy Ghost to help us pray. Because he is the third person of the God Head, we can be assured that he will not lead us in a deceitful way. We can trust his judgments.

> *"Likewise the Spirit also helpeth our infirmities: for we know not what we should pray for as we ought: but the Spirit itself maketh intercession for us with groanings which cannot be uttered. And he that searcheth the hearts knoweth what is the mind of the Spirit because he maketh intercession for the saints according to the will of God. And we know that all things work together for good to them that love God, to them who are the called according to his purpose." Romans 8: 26-28*

> *VERSE FORTY-FOUR AND FORTY-FIVE:* *"So shall I keep thy law continually for ever and ever And I will walk at liberty: for I seek thy precepts."*

This indicates our purpose to do it, and have the assurance that we will do it, if God should enable us to retain even the slightest hold on the truth.

The Word continually is the key word in this promise. We must study the Word daily instead of just reading a devotional book written by some good writer. The Word of God is a living book that speaks to our spirit as we intensely study it. Words that normally don't seem important to us jump off the page through the power of the Holy Ghost who joys in leading us into all truth.

Once again, we are admonished by the apostle Paul who stated to Timothy and you and me in the 21st century:

> *"Study to shew thyself approved unto God, a workman that needeth not to be ashamed, rightly dividing the word of truth. But shun profane and vain babblings: for they will increase unto more ungodliness." 2 Timothy 2: 15-16*

> *VERSE FORTY-SIX: "I will speak of thy testimonies also before kings, and will not be ashamed."*

When I stand before an audience, I always pray to be hidden behind the cross, not because I am afraid, but that the people may see the reason for the message of the hour. I am nothing without the anointing of the Holy Ghost.

This kind of peace only comes to a preacher or teacher who has spent hours in study and prayer before the presentation of the message is given.

> *"By humility and the fear of the LORD are riches, and honour, and life." Proverbs 22: 4*

> *VERSE FORTY-SEVEN: "And I will delight myself in thy commandments, which I have loved."*

If I have studied and prayed for the message or lesson and I know the message is an anointed message from God, I feel like the Lord is standing with me in the pulpit.

If I am at a church that God has opened the door, I have learned not to look upon the faces of the congregation, unless the Holy Ghost instructs me to do so.

"Thou therefore gird up thy loins, and arise, and speak unto them all that I command thee: be not dismayed at their faces, lest I confound thee before them." Jerimiah 1: 17

<u>VERSE FORTY-EIGHT</u>: *"My hands also will I lift up unto thy commandments, which I have loved; and I will meditate in thy statutes."*

Private prayer and praise are a must when one is a preacher or teacher. The lifting up ourselves to God shows total surrender to his purpose for our ministry. We are not called to bring shame to the kingdom, only promotion of our blessed redeemer who is the living Son of God.

"…for the joy of the Lord is your strength." Nehemiah 8: 10

UNIT SEVEN:
ZAIN
Psalm 119: 49-56

VERSE FORTY-NINE: *"Remember the word unto thy servant, upon which thou hast caused me to hope."*

As I read this verse, my mind went to the many times I was in a quandary about which way I would turn. I also remembered the way God would speak to me though a still small voice, *"Just trust me."* There were times when I was tested and tried; I never lost my hope, even when my faith waivered.

"The LORD is the portion of mine inheritance and of my cup: thou maintainest my lot. The lines are fallen unto me in pleasant places; yea, I have a goodly heritage. I will bless the LORD, who hath given me counsel: my reins also instruct me in the night seasons. I have set the LORD always before me: because he is at my right hand, I shall not be moved. Therefore my heart is glad, and my glory rejoiceth: my flesh also shall rest in hope." Psalm 16: 5-9

VERSE FIFTY: *"This is my comfort in my affliction: for thy word hath quickened me."*

How thankful I am for the presence of the Holy Ghost in my life. In times of physical and spiritual pain, the Holy Ghost moves in my spirit and helps me! How great is the trinity! How great is the living Word of God; it is the anchor of truth in the midst of confusion!

> *"For the eyes of the Lord are over the righteous, and his ears are open unto their prayers: but the face of the Lord is against them that do evil. And who is he that will harm you, if ye be followers of that which is good? But and if ye suffer for righteousness' sake, happy are ye: and be not afraid of their terror, neither be troubled; But sanctify the Lord God in your hearts: and be ready always to give an answer to every man that asketh you a reason of the hope that is in you with meekness and fear: Having a good conscience; that, whereas they speak evil of you, as of evildoers, they may be ashamed that falsely accuse your good conversation in Christ. For it is better, if the will of God be so, that ye suffer for well doing, than for evil doing. For Christ also hath once suffered for sins, the just for the unjust, that he might bring us to God, being put to death in the flesh, but quickened by the Spirit:" 1 Peter 3: 12-18*

Let me always be found praising my Father in Heaven for his everlasting love and care and pray that many who are struggling will experience his presence in their lives, both those who are in sin and those who have been Christians for many years. May we have a love feast with our Father!

<u>*VERSE FIFTY-ONE:*</u> *"The proud have had me greatly in derision: yet have I not declined from thy law."*

Derision is a tool Satan uses very often against many believers. The proud of this world who disregard the Word of God are growing stronger every day because they are being deceived by Satan to believe this is the only life they have. They scoff and laugh at right and accept the wrong. Sometimes we as Christians are persecuted and tempted as Jeremiah was in chapter 20: verses 1-13. But if we love as God loves, we will not decline in ministry; there still are those who will hear, we just have to try harder to find them.

> *"This second epistle, beloved, I now write unto you; in both which I stir up your pure minds by way of remembrance: That ye may be mindful of the words which were spoken before by the holy prophets, and of the commandment of us the apostles of the Lord and Saviour.*

Knowing this first, here is the promise of his coming? for since the fathers fell asleep, all things continue as they were from the beginning of the creation. For this they willingly are ignorant of, that by the word of God the heavens were of old, and the earth standing out of the water and in the water: Whereby the world that then was, being overflowed with water, perished: But the heavens and the earth, which are now, by the same word are kept in store, reserved unto fire against the day of judgment and perdition of ungodly men. But, beloved, be not ignorant of this one thing, that one day is with the Lord as a thousand years, and a thousand years as one day. The Lord is not slack concerning his promise, as some men count slack-ness; but is longsuffering to us-ward, not willing that any should perish, but that all should come to repentance. But the day of the Lord will come as a thief in the night; in the which the heavens shall pass away with a great noise, and the elements shall melt with fervent heat, the earth also and the works that are therein shall be burned up. Seeing then that all these things shall be dissolved, what manner of persons ought ye to be in all holy conversation and godliness, Looking for and hasting unto the coming of the day of God, wherein the heavens being on fire shall be dissolved, and the elements shall melt with fervent heat? Nevertheless we, according to his promise, look for new heavens and a new earth, where in dwelleth righteousness. Wherefore beloved, seeing that ye look for much things, be diligent that ye may be found of him in peace, without spot, and blameless." 2 Peter 3: 1-14

<u>*VERSE FIFTY-TWO:*</u> *"I remembered thy judgments of old, O LORD; and have comforted myself."*

We as born again by the Spirit Christians must remember God is a God of order. His judgments are perfect; he is always just and fair. His love is everlasting even though men are not perfect and reject him; his hand is always extended.

When I am troubled concerning the times we live in, I depend heavily upon the comfort of the Holy Ghost. He is always near to those who are seeking truth. I also find much comfort in reading the 23rd Psalm.

"The LORD is my shepherd; I shall not want. He maketh me to lie down in green pastures: he leadeth me beside the still waters.

<u>*VERSE FIFTY-THREE:*</u> *"Horror hath taken hold upon me because of the wicked that forsake thy law."*

Sometimes I think about Hell and what I vision is going to happen to those who reject our Savior. I shudder to think of an eternity of torment, plus the aloneness one will feel, the memories that may be in their mind of when they were offered salvation and wished they could live their life over again.

I think of the account of the rich man and Lazarus. The rich man being in torment and saw Abraham afar off and Lazarus in his bosom; oh, how he must have felt at the rebuke Abraham gave him concerning his request.

I see people rebelling against God every day willingly exposing themselves to God's wrath. Their conduct alarms me. Their danger appalls me. Their condition overwhelms me.

My prayer at this point is: *"Lord, give me more compassion and help me reach them some way before it is too late. Amen!"*

<u>*VERSE FIFTY-FOUR:*</u> *"Thy statutes have been my songs in the house of my pilgrimage."*

As I walk with my Lord, I never forget where I was when he found me, and how he restored me from myself and made me into a new creation. He delivered me from human heredities that doomed me. He is most gracious to me. How can I ever repay him? The fact is, I can't; all he desires from me is to honor and love him as my Father as I accept his wonderful, loving, unspeakable gift of salvation through his Son's blood sacrifice.

"I waited patiently for the LORD; and he inclined unto me, and heard my cry. He brought me up also out of an horrible pit, out of

the miry clay, and set my feet upon a rock, and established and fear, and shall trust in the LORD. Blessed is that man that maketh the LORD his trust, and respecteth not the proud, nor such as turn aside to lies. Many, O LORD my God, are thy wonderful works which thou hast done, and thy thoughts which are to us-ward: they cannot be reckoned up in order unto thee: if I would declare and speak of them, they are more than can be numbered. Sacrifice and offering thou didst not desire; mine ears hast thou opened: burnt offering and sin offering hast thou not required." Psalm 40: 1-6

VERSE FIFTY-FIVE AND FIFTY-SIX: "I have remembered thy name, O LORD, in the night, and have kept thy law. This I had, because I kept thy precepts."

Lord, help me not to use the Word I love so much in vanity; help me think upon thy name night and day and keep your Word in faith. Help me continue committing all to thee.

"Fret not thyself because of evildoers, neither be thou envious against the workers of iniquity. For they shall soon be cut down like the grass, and wither as the green herb. Trust in the LORD, and do good; so shalt thou dwell in the land, and verily thou shalt be fed. Delight thyself also in the LORD; and he shall give thee the desires of thine heart. Commit thy way unto the LORD; trust also in him; and he shall bring it to pass. And he shall bring forth thy righteousness as the light, and thy judgment as the noonday. Rest in the LORD, and wait patiently for him: fret not thyself because of him who prospereth in his way, because of the man who bringeth wicked devices to pass. Cease from anger, and forsake wrath: fret not thyself in any wise to do evil. For evildoers shall be cut off: but those that wait upon the LORD, they shall inherit the earth. For yet a little while, and the wicked shall not be: yea, thou shalt diligently consider his place, and it shall not be. But the meek shall inherit the earth; and shall delight themselves in the abundance of peace." Psalm 37: 1-11

Fretting never accomplishes anything, but praising our Father in Heaven is the way to keep the joy bells ringing in our heart.

UNIT EIGHT:

CHETH
Psalm 119: 57-64

VERSE FIFTY-SEVEN: _"Thou art my portion, O LORD: I have said that I would keep thy words."_

God is to me what other people seek in wealth, honor, pleasure, and fame. God is my all and in all. I have found my purpose in living; my mind and spirit are settled. I desire to obey him and keep his commandments. But you know we human beings must keep ourselves following the lead of the Holy Ghost to accomplish this goal. It is a fight of faith not an artificial fix.

"My heart is fixed, O God, my heart is fixed: I will sing and give praise." Psalm 57: 7

"O God, my heart is fixed; I will sing and give praise, even with my glory." Psalm 108: 1

VERSE FIFTY-EIGHT: _"I intreated thy favour with my whole heart: be merciful unto me according to thy word."_

My prayer for my life is that my focus will be upon him and his Word in order for my countenance to show forth his glory. My desire is to always be sincere in my affection toward my Father and his Son in order to enjoy his grace and mercy until my final day upon this earth.

"We have heard with our ears, O God, our fathers have told us, what work thou didst in their days, in the times of old. How thou didst drive out the heathen with thy hand, and plantedst them; how thou didst afflict the people, and cast them out. For they got not the land in possession by their own sword, neither did their own arm save them: but thy right hand, and thine arm, and the light of thy countenance, because thou hadst a favour push down our enemies: through thy name will we tread them under that rise up against us. For I will not trust in my bow, neither shall my sword save me. But thou hast saved us from our enemies, and hast put them to shame that hated us. In God we boast all the day long, and praise thy name for ever. Selah." Psalm 44: 1-8

<u>*VERSE FIFTY-NINE*</u>: *"I thought on my ways, and turned my feet unto thy testimonies."*

In my private times with the Lord, I take a look at my life to see if indeed I am doing what I profess. Many times in the course of the day, we can be caught in conversations, etc., and if we are not careful, we can say the wrong things. Even through our body language we can project the wrong impressions.

I have heard many confessing professing Christians make the statement, *"Oh, I don't worry about what I do or say because God knows my heart."* Yes, in fact he does. Our hearts can lead us astray.

"The heart is deceitful above all things, and desperately wicked: who can know it? I the LORD search the heart, I try the reins, even to give every man according to his ways, and according to the fruit of his doings." Jeremiah 17: 9, 10

<u>*VERSE SIXTY*</u>: *"I made haste, and delayed not to keep thy commandments."*

When we feel a slipping in our experience with the Lord, the Holy Ghost will cause an urgent feeling in our spirit; when this happens, we should immediately check our standing with the Lord.

Many Christians gradually slip away from the Lord because they have hardened their hearts and conformed to the hunger of the flesh instead of conforming to the image of God's son. Sometimes they get comfortable in that state and modify their knowledge of the Word to fit their situation instead of repenting.

> *"Take heed brethren, lest there be in any of you an evil heart of unbelief, in departing from the living God. But exhort one another daily, while it is called To day; lest any of you be hardened through the deceitfulness of sin. For we are made partakers of Christ, if we hold the beginning of our confidence stedfast unto the end; While it is said, Today if ye will hear his voice, harden not your hearts, as in the provocation. For some, when they had heard, did provoke: howbeit not all that came out of Egypt by Moses. But with whom was he grieved forty years? Was it not with them that had sinned, whose carcases fell in the wilderness? And to whom sware he that they should not enter into his rest, but to them that believed not? So we see that they could not enter in because of unbelief." Hebrews 3: 12-19*

> *VERSE SIXTY-ONE:* *"The bands of the wicked have robbed me: but I have not forgotten thy law."*

The enemy of our soul will use anything to try to become prisoners of a modern society, a modern way of worship, if you please, in order to deceive and nullify our faith in God.

Beware of smooth words coming from the pulpit, there is a Heaven to gain and Hell to avoid. Praise God, Jesus paid the price for our sins; let us always run back to the Word of God to verify what is being preached in the pulpits of America. If a message comes from the pulpit that promotes anyone except the Holy Trinity, let us beware!

> *"My son, if thou wilt receive my words, and hide my commandments with thee; So that thou incline thine ear unto wisdom, and apply thine heart to understanding; Yea, if thou criest after knowledge, and liftest up thy voice for understanding; If thou seekest her as silver, and searchest for her as for hid treasures; Then shalt thou understand the fear of the LORD, and find the knowledge of God. For the LORD giveth wisdom: out of his mouth cometh knowledge and understanding. He layeth up sound wisdom for the righteous:*

VERSE SIXTY-TWO: *"At midnight I will rise to give thanks unto thee because of thy righteous judgments."*

In the quiet hours of the night before I retire is my favorite time to pray, reflect and study.

Jesus did both, but it seems the early morning was more favorable to him. It really does not matter what the hour of the day is. Daniel prayed in the morning, at noon and at night. The point is: find a place and a time where you can be quiet before the Lord and hear his still small voice and understand his loving kindness and righteous judgments.

"I cried with my whole heart; hear me, O LORD: I will keep thy statutes. I cried unto thee; save me, and I shall keep thy testimonies. I prevented the dawning of the morning, and cried: I hoped in thy word. Mine eyes prevent the night watches that I might meditate in thy word. Hear my voice according unto thy lovingkindness: O LORD, quicken me according to thy judgment." Psalm 119: 145-149

VERSE SIXTY-THREE: *"I am a companion of all them that fear thee and of them that keep thy precepts."*

It is a good practice to fellowship with your fellow ministers and layman who are faithful followers of God. Personally, I draw much strength and encouragement with those I fellowship with. Actually, we are known by the company we keep.

We also are an encouragement to each other when we are not afraid to exhort each other if there are problems in our lives. We can do this because we each have the love of Christ in our hearts and desire to live a righteous lifestyle and please God. There is a warning however; we must never form clicks and become self-righteous.

"Blessed is the man that walketh not in the counsel of the ungodly, nor standeth in the way of sinners, nor sitteth in the seat of the

scornful. But his delight is in the law of the LORD; and in his law doth he meditate day and night. And he shall be like a tree planted by the rivers of water, that bringeth forth his fruit in his season; his leaf also shall not wither; and what-soever he doeth shall prosper. The ungodly are not so: but are like the chaff which the wind driveth away. Therefore the ungodly shall not stand in the judgment, nor sinners in the congregation of the righteous. For the LORD knoweth the way of the righteous: but the way of the ungodly shall perish." Psalm 1: 1-6

<u>*VERSE SIXTY-FOUR:*</u> *"The earth, O LORD, is full of thy mercy: teach me thy statutes"*

Those who focus upon God daily have full proof of his goodness, patience and compassion. The only way one can appreciate what he does for us each day is to prepare our heart properly through study of the Word and praise, then show his love to all who you come in contact. Many try to fake it and wind up depressed. True love as a born again by the Spirit Christian is to radiate God's glory, not rushing up to a person and pretending to love them, but to truly show it by caring for them. We are to keep his statutes and obey them when the Holy Ghost opens an occasion to do so. Until then, just show your care for people by being courteous and pleasant.

"Blessed is the people that know the joyful sound: they shall walk, O LORD, in the light of thy countenance. In thy name shall they rejoice all the day: and in thy righteousness shall they be exalted. For thou art the glory of their strength: and in thy favour our horn shall be exalted. For the LORD is our defence; and the Holy One of Israel is our king." Psalm 89: 15-18

"Rejoice in the Lord always: and again I say, Rejoice. Let your moderation be known unto all men. The Lord is at hand." Philippians 4: 4, 5

UNIT NINE:
TETH
Psalm 119: 65-72

<u>*VERSE SIXTY-FIVE:*</u> *"Thou hast dealt well with thy servant, O LORD, according unto thy word."*

I have been dealt with by the Lord according to his Word many times both good and bad. I have been blessed beyond measure even when I had to be disciplined by the Word.

It is kind of like a child who has done good or bad and the parent has dealt with their child accordingly. The end result is good. Our love and faith in our Father are strengthened because truth has prevailed.

> *"Let, I pray thee, thy merciful kindness be for my comfort, according to thy word unto thy servant. Let thy tender mercies come unto me, that I may live: for thy law is my delight. Let the proud be ashamed; for they dealt perversely with me without a cause: but I will meditate in thy precepts. Let those that fear thee turn unto me, and those that have known thy testimonies. Let my heart be sound in thy statutes; that I be not ashamed." Psalm 119: 76-80*

<u>*VERSE SIXTY-SIX:*</u> *"Teach me good judgment and knowledge: for I have believed thy commandments."*

The word here rendered *judgment* means *taste*. It is the power by which we determine the quality of things as sweet, bitter, sour, etc. Then *judgment* is applied to our mind or understanding, by which we determine the moral quality of things, or decide what is right or wrong; wise or foolish; good or evil. Here it means that Solomon desired to have full exercise the of appreciating what is right and of distinguishing it from what is wrong.

We know the commandments of Jesus in Matthew 22; 37-40; when we put them into practice, we begin to really know what they mean and we become kinder and more pleasant. We know his will and doctrine and put it into practice.

"To give knowledge of salvation unto his people by the remission of their sins, Through the tender mercy of our God; whereby the dayspring from on high hath visited us, To give light to them that sit in darkness and in the shadow of death, to guide our feet into the way of peace." Luke 1: 77-79

<u>*VERSE SIXTY-SEVEN*</u>: *"Before I was afflicted I went astray: but now have I kept thy word."*

The book of James gives instruction to those who suffer afflictions. Afflictions do not mean illness or maladies; they usually mean trials. Trials are sent to us many times to humble our heart in order for God to really communicate. James teaches, *"Is any among you afflicted? Let him pray."* That statement seems rather cold and uncaring, but when we are in a trial, usually there is no one but the Lord to help us because it may be a trial to lead one closer to the Father. We humans are designed to care more in the physical realm instead of the spiritual realm with afflictions. We try to counsel, but many times we fail. Sometimes the trial is very personal and must be worked out in private prayer.

The afflicted must bear the truth and come to terms with their Father through the ministry of the Holy Ghost and the correct care of Jesus who has been tempted in all points as all humans. It is best for us to pray for them from afar.

"Seeing then that we have a great high priest, that is passed into the heavens, Jesus the Son of God, let us hold fast our profession. For we have not an high priest which cannot be touched with the

feeling of our infirmities; but was in all points tempted like as we are, yet without sin. Let us therefore come boldly unto the throne of grace that we may obtain mercy and find grace to help in time of need." Hebrews 4: 14-16

<u>*VERSE SIXTY-EIGHT:*</u> *"Thou art good, and doest good; teach me thy statutes."*

God's goodness is not just a common goodness. It is filled with active loving acts toward his people. Even in his righteous judgment there is goodness that promotes the happiness and fulfilment of those who are born again by the Spirit. Also, it is because of his goodness and mercies that the human race still remains upon this Earth and receives his call to whosoever will believe upon his Son shall be saved from utter destruction.

We too should pray and follow the leading of the Holy Ghost to become more acquainted with his word!

"Fear not, little flock; for it is your Father's good pleasure to give you the kingdom. Sell that ye have, and give alms; provide yourselves bags which wax not old, a treasure in the heavens that faileth not, where no thief approacheth, neither moth corrupteth. For where your treasure is, there will your heart be also. Let your loins be girded about, and your lights burning; And ye yourselves like unto men that wait for their lord, when he will return from the wedding; that when he cometh and knocketh, they may open unto him immediately. Blessed are those servants, whom the lord when he cometh shall find watching: verily I say unto you, that he shall gird himself, and make them to sit down to meat, and will come forth and serve them. And if he shall come in the second watch, or come in the third watch, and find them so, blessed are those servants. And this know, that if the goodman of the house had known what hour the thief would come, he would have watched, and not have suffered his house to be broken through. Be ye therefore ready also: for the Son of man cometh at an hour when ye think not." Luke 12: 32-40

<u>*VERSE SIXTY-NINE:*</u> *"The proud have forged a lie against me: but I will keep thy precepts with my whole heart."*

I have been among people in the world and in the church who exalt themselves in pride and spread untruths concerning my person and conduct. These things hurt me severely when I did not know the Word well enough to ignore such things. I have seen God come to my defense many times even when I did not act with wisdom and tried to defend myself. The grace and mercy of God is great and wonderful to us when we are ignorant, *if* we will depend upon him to be our advocate not only to God, but to human kind. Thank God, I have been repaid time and time again for wrongs that have done to me.

The secret I discovered though trials of life is to stay true to my Father and depend upon my advocate Jesus Christ to fight my battles for me in the Holy Court of heaven.

> *"For we wrestle not against flesh and blood, but against principalities, against powers, against the rulers of the darkness of this world, against spiritual wickedness in high places; Wherefore take unto you the whole armour of God, that ye may be able to withstand in the evil day, and having done all, to stand. Stand therefore, having your loins girt about with truth, and having on the breastplate of righteousness; And your feet shod with the preparation of the gospel of peace; Above all, taking the shield of faith, wherewith ye shall be able to quench all the fiery darts of the wicked. And take the helmet of salvation, and the sword of the Spirit, which is the word of God: Praying always with all prayer and supplication in the Spirit, and watching thereunto with all perseverance and supplication for all saints;" Ephesians 6: 12-18*

THE ONLY FIGHT WE ARE TO BE IN IS THE GOOD FIGHT OF FAITH! 1 Timothy 6: 12; 2 Timothy 4: 7

VERSE SEVENTY: *"Their heart is as fat as grease; but I delight in thy law."*

Many today really believe they can live like they want to and be accepted into Heaven because they have goodness, wealth and charity here on Earth. But what counts is what is recorded in Heaven on their page.

We as born again by the Spirit Christians are privileged to have the Holy Ghost to help us not only learn the scriptures but to enjoy doing so, thereby conforming to the image of Christ!

<u>*VERSE SEVENTY-ONE*</u>: *"It is good for me that I have been af-flicted; that I might learn thy statutes."*

At the time of afflictions, it is not comfortable or enjoyable. But in retrospect, all of the afflictions I have been through have prospered me spiritually and financially. I have a peace that passes all understanding. But be it known, I had rather have no more afflictions! Thus, I will learn more of God's Word and apply it to my life and lifestyle.

> *"Father, I boast only in you! Help me to be an encourager to those who may be going through afflictions because you have given me understanding. Amen."*

> <u>*VERSE SEVENTY-TWO*</u>: *"The law of thy mouth is better unto me than thousands of gold and silver."*

My wife has a phrase she uses occasionally: *"Let the Holy Ghost step on my tongue."* I believe we would all be better witnesses for Christ if we would pray the following:

> *"LORD, I cry unto thee: make haste unto me; give ear unto my voice, when I cry unto thee. Let my prayer be set forth before thee as incense; and the lifting up of my hands as the evening sacrifice. Set a watch, O LORD, before my mouth; keep the door of my lips. In-cline not my heart to any evil thing, to practice wicked works with men that work iniquity: and let me not eat of their dainties. Let the righteous smite me; it shall be a kindness: and let him reprove me; it shall be an excellent oil which shall not break my head: for yet my prayer also shall be in their calamities." Psalm 141: 1-5*

REMEMBER THE FOLLOWING SAYING: *"A closed mouth gathers no foot!"*

UNIT TEN:

JOD
Psalm 119: 73-80

VERSE SEVENTY-THREE "*Thy hands have made me and fashioned me: give me understanding, that I may learn thy commandments.*"

Sometimes I wonder why God made me. What did he have in mind when he fashioned me the way he did? Why couldn't I have been taller and slimmer? Why is my hair falling out? These, of course, are ridiculous questions.

As we humans grow up and mature, we follow our natural instincts and wander far from God's purpose for our life instead of seeking God's guidance.

But we discover why God made us just the way we are when we become born again by the Spirit. We become a new person; we still look the same, but a miraculous thing has happened! We have returned to the potter's wheel, then he begins to form his original plan by giving us understanding as we digest it and learn his Word and not only begin to be productive, but fulfilling his will, not ours.

"If I say, Surely the darkness shall cover me; even the night shall be light about me. Yea, the darkness hideth not from thee; but the night shineth as the day: the darkness and the light are both alike to thee. For thou hast possessed my reins: thou hast covered me in my mother's womb. I will praise thee; for I am fearfully and won-

derfully made: marvellous are thy works; and that my soul knoweth right well. My substance was not hid from thee, when I was made in secret, and curiously wrought in the lowest parts of the earth. Thine eyes did see my substance, yet being un-perfect; and in thy book all my members were written, which in continuance were fashioned, when as yet there was none of them. How precious also are thy thoughts unto me, O God; how great is the sum of them! If I should count them, they are more in number than the sand: when I awake, I am still with thee." Psalm 139: 11-18

My prayer in my declining years is: *"Spirit of the living God, Spirit of the living God, fall fresh on me; melt me, mold me, fill me; Spirit of the living God, fall fresh on me!"*

<u>*VERSE SEVENTY-FOUR:*</u> *"They that fear thee will be glad when they see me; because I have hoped in thy word."*

My desire for those who I am acquainted with and serve with is that they will see Jesus in me. Not just in works but in an attitude fashioned by God himself!

I pray they will welcome me into their fellowship and regard and treat me as a friend and brother. Wicked men are men of the world and do not value that kind of fellowship. They are satisfied with the friendship of those who, like themselves, have no fear of God. The friendship of those who love God is of more value than that of any others. Let us as born again by the Spirit Christians live a life in front of those who do not know Christ in order to cause them to desire to have that kind of fellowship.

My hope is totally founded by what thus saith the Lord God!

"A man that hath friends must shew himself friendly: and there is a friend that sticketh closer than a brother." Proverbs 18: 24

"Greater love hath no man than this: that a man lay down his life for his friends. Ye are my friends, if ye do whatsoever I command you. Henceforth I call you not servants; for the servant knoweth not what his lord doeth: but I have called you friends; for all things that I have heard of my Father I have made known unto you." John 15:13-15

<u>VERSE SEVENTY-FIVE</u>: *"I know, O LORD, that thy judgments are right, and that thou in faithfulness hast afflicted me."*

We know God's judgments are correct; however, they are mysterious at times and sometimes hard to bear. The trials that come our way many times seem unfair, but we know they are allowed at times for a divine purpose.

One of the greatest things I have learned in my walk with God is he knows what is right and wrong in me and loves me enough to send tests to humble my heart to the point of readjusting my direction. He desires for us to be happy in his righteousness so he can shower us with his blessings.

"Beloved, I wish above all things that thou mayest prosper and be in health, <u>even as thy soul prospereth.</u>" 3rd John verse 2

<u>VERSE SEVENTY-SIX</u>: *Let, I pray thee, thy merciful kindness be for my comfort, according to thy word unto thy servant."*

It is a wonderful thing to know God and realize he desires to be kind and merciful to us all the time. But many times God's merciful kindness is a conditional blessing. What we are doing and involved in must be according to his Word not our will.

"I will say of the LORD, He is my refuge and my fortress: my God; in him will I trust. Surely he shall deliver thee from the snare of the fowler, and from the noisome pestilence. He shall cover thee with his feathers, and under his wings shalt thou trust: his truth shall be thy shield and buckler. Thou shalt not be afraid for the terror by night; nor for the arrow that flieth by day; Nor for the pestilence that walketh in darkness; nor for the destruction that wasteth at noonday." Psalm 91: 2-6

"Thy word have I hid in mine heart, that I might not sin against thee. Blessed art thou, O LORD: teach me thy statutes." Psalm 119: 11, 12

<u>VERSE SEVENTY-SEVEN</u>: *"Let thy tender mercies come unto me, that I may live: for thy law is my delight."*

I am happy and blessed by the Lord's tender mercies I have enjoyed through the years of my life. Without them, I would be in Hell today. When I was born again by the Spirit, I felt love like I had never experienced. Afterwards, I made some unwise discussions, preached some things that were wrong during my life and yet his mercy sustained me. I believe the only reason he put up with me is because I was created in his image and he did not want to be embarrassed so he guided me into the real truth of his Word through the ministry of the Holy Ghost, and it has become a joy to me and filled me with more hunger to fellowship with my heavenly Father.

> *"O give thanks unto the LORD; for he is good: for his mercy endureth for ever. O give thanks unto the God of gods: for his mercy endureth for ever. O give thanks to the Lord of lords: for his mercy endureth for ever. To him who alone doeth great wonders: for his mercy endureth for ever. To him that by wisdom made the heavens: for his mercy endureth for ever. To him that stretched out the earth above the waters: for his mercy endureth for ever. To him that made great lights: for his mercy endureth for ever: The sun to rule by day: for his mercy endureth for ever The moon and stars to rule by night: for his mercy endureth for ever. To him that smote Egypt in their firstborn: for his mercy endureth for ever: And brought out Israel from among them: for his mercy endureth for ever: With a strong hand, and with a stretched out arm: for his mercy endureth for ever. To him which divided the Red sea into parts: for his mercy endureth for ever: And made Israel to pass through the midst of it: for his mercy endureth for ever: But overthrew Pharaoh and his host in the Red sea: for his mercy endureth for ever. To him which led his people through the wilderness: for his mercy endureth for ever. To him which smote great kings: for his mercy endureth for ever: And slew famous kings: for his mercy endureth for ever: Sihon king of the Amorites: for his mercy endureth for ever: And Og the king of Bashan: for his mercy endureth for ever: And gave their land for an heritage: for his mercy endureth for ever: Even an heritage unto Israel his servant: for his mercy endureth for ever. Who remembered us in our low estate: for his mercy endureth for ever: And hath redeemed us from our enemies: for his mercy endureth for ever. Who giveth food to all flesh: for his mercy endureth for ever. O give thanks unto the God of heaven: for his mercy endureth for ever." Psalm 136: 1-26*

<u>VERSE SEVENTY-EIGHT</u>: *"Let the proud be ashamed; for they dealt perversely with me without a cause: but I will meditate in thy precepts."*

Pride is one of the most dangerous attributes a minister of the gospel can experience. Pride not only makes one ashamed, it can also destroy his or her influence as a spiritual leader. Pride will lead one to say and do things without thinking about the consequences.

One of the greatest days of my life is when the Lord spoke to me concerning my pride and disciplined me severely! Since that time, I learned to meditate on the truth of the Word and allow the Holy Ghost to guide my conversation.

"The highway of the upright is to depart from evil: he that keepeth his way preserveth his soul. Pride goeth before destruction, and an haughty spirit before a fall. Better it is to be of an humble spirit with the lowly, than to divide the spoil with the proud. He that handleth a matter wisely shall find good: and whoso trusteth in the LORD, happy is he. The wise in heart shall be called prudent: and the sweetness of the lips increaseth learning. Understanding is a wellspring of life unto him that hath it: but the instruction of fools is folly. The heart of the wise teacheth his mouth, and addeth learning to his lips." Proverbs 16: 17-23

<u>*VERSE SEVENTY-NINE:*</u> *"Let those that fear thee turn unto me, and those that have known thy testimonies."*

A healthy fear for God is something that is not seen much in the 21st century. I thank God for the ministers I have fellowship with who have a reverent fear for God. Their living testimonies prove their allegiance to our Father in Heaven. They appreciate the beauty of the commandments of God is the common ground of Christian friendship through the Lord Jesus Christ.

I love what Spurgeon said about Christian fellowship:

"Some Christians try to go to heaven alone, in solitude. But believers are not compared to bears or lions or other animals that wander alone. Those who belong to Christ are sheep in this respect; that they love to get together. Sheep go in flocks, and so do God's people.

"Be ye not unequally yoked together with unbelievers: for what fel-lowship hath righteousness with unrighteousness? and what com-munion hath light with darkness? And what concord hath Christ with Belial? or what part hath he that believeth with an infidel? And what agree-ment hath the temple of God with idols? for ye are the temple of the living God; as God hath said, I will dwell in them, and walk in them; and I will be their God, and they shall be my people. Wherefore come out from among them, and be ye separate, saith the Lord, and touch not the unclean thing; and I will receive you, And will be a Father unto you, and ye shall be my sons and daughters, saith the Lord Almighty." 2 Corinthians 6: 14-18

<u>VERSE EIGHTY:</u> *"Let my heart be sound in thy statutes; that I be not ashamed."*

When our life finally becomes established or fixed upon God's Holy Word, our hearts desire is to walk in the righteousness of Christ and have no improper attachment to the world.

Christians have no occasion to be ashamed of a pure heart; he or she should shout hallelujah to God for making them whole and pure. We are not to boast, but humbly present ourselves to becoming righteous in the sight of God through the blood of Jesus the Christ, not self-rightness!

"The earth is the LORD's, and the fullness thereof; the world, and they that dwell therein. For he hath founded it upon the seas and established it upon the floods. Who shall ascend into the hill of the LORD? or who shall stand in his holy place? He that hath clean hands and a pure heart; who hath not lifted up his soul unto vanity, nor sworn deceitfully. He shall receive the blessing from the LORD, and righteousness from the God of his salvation. This is the gener-ation of them that seek him, that seek thy face, O Jacob. Selah. Lift up your head, O ye gates; and be ye lift up, ye everlasting doors; and the King of glory shall come in. Who is this King of glory? The LORD strong and mighty, the LORD mighty in battle. Lift up your heads, O ye gates; even lift them up, ye everlasting doors; and the King of glory shall come in. Who is this King of glory? The LORD of hosts, he is the King of glory. Selah." Psalm 24: 1-10

UNIT ELEVEN:

CAPH
Psalm 119: 81-88

VERSE EIGHTY-ONE: "*My soul fainteth for thy salvation: but I hope in thy word.*"

There are times when I think of my personal salvation, my thoughts wander, and I am tempted to look back at my past. When this happens, my heart gives way, and I begin to think, how can God wipe away all the past sins and freely give me salvation? It is then that I look toward Heaven and begin to offer a sacrifice of praise [Jeremiah 33: 11] until my spirit again focuses upon my Father's grace and mercy by coming to Earth in the form of human flesh; was tempted in all points as we are and overcame them with three statements from the Word of God. It is then my trust in God increases and I am encouraged in my faith by wholly relying upon the Word of faith!

"I will lift up mine eyes unto the hills, from whence cometh my help. My help cometh from the LORD, which made heaven and earth. He will not suffer thy foot to be moved: he that keepeth thee will not slumber. Behold, he that keepeth Israel shall neither slumber nor sleep. The LORD is thy keeper: the LORD is thy shade upon thy right hand. The sun shall not smite thee by day, nor the moon by night. The LORD shall preserve thee from all evil: he shall preserve thy soul. The LORD shall preserve thy going out and

thy coming in from this time forth, and even for evermore." Psalm
121: 1-8

*"…without faith it is impossible to please him: for he that cometh
to God must believe that he is, and that he is a rewarder of them
that diligently seek him."* Hebrews 11:6

<u>VERSE EIGHTY-TWO:</u> *"Mine eyes fail for thy word, saying,
When wilt thou comfort me?"*

A few years ago, I had a very severe problem with my heart racing; it was
exhausting me physically, and I thought I was near death. I did not fear death,
but I was fearful of the transition. One night I could not sleep so I read the
Psalms through several times. Then around dawn, the fear completely left me,
and I rested a couple of days in that blessing and my heart regulated. It was if
God let me know all was well and no matter what happened everything was
okay! He comforted me through the power of the Holy Ghost. Now, I am
looking forward to the transition!

I believe God allows us to go through tough times to remind us he is in
control of our lives, and we can trust him.

*"How precious also are thy thoughts unto me, O God! How great
is the sum of them! If I should count them, they are more in number
than the sand: when I awake, I am still with thee."* Psalm 139:
17, 18

*"Behold, I shew you a mystery; We shall not all sleep, but we shall
all be changed, In a moment, in the twinkling of an eye, at the
last trump: for the trumpet shall sound, and the dead shall be
raised incorruptible, and we shall be changed. For this corruptible
must put on incorruption, and this mortal must put on immortality. So when this corruptible shall have put on incorruption,
and this mortal shall have put on immortality, then shall be
brought to pass the saying that is written, Death is swallowed up
in victory. O death, where is thy sting? O grave, where is thy victory? The sting of death is sin; and the strength of sin is the law.
But thanks be to God, which giveth us the victory through our
Lord Jesus Christ. Therefore, my beloved brethren, be ye steadfast, unmovable, always abounding in the work of the Lord, for-*

asmuch as ye know that your labour is not in vain in the Lord."
1 Corinthians 15: 51-58

*VERSE EIGHTY-THREE: "For I am become like a bottle in the
smoke; yet do I not forget thy statutes."*

If we are not careful, we can become like the bottles that were made of
skins in biblical times that would become dry as they hung in the tents where
the smoke of their fires would dry them out and lose their elasticity and what
was in them would leak out.

A truly born again by the Spirit Christian will be sustained in these times
if we will continue to remember God's promises have never failed us. Our ves-
sels will never become inflexible and still if we will be living sacrifices unto
God.

> *"Ye are the light of the world. A city that is set on a hill cannot be
> hid.; Neither do men light a candle and put it under a bushel, but
> on a candlestick; and it giveth light unto all that are in the house.
> Let your light so shine before men, that they may see your good
> works and glorify your Father which is in heaven." Matthew 5:
> 14-16*

> *"That every one of you should know how to possess his vessel in sanc-
> tification and honour." 1 Thessalonians 4: 4*

> *VERSE EIGHTY-FOUR: "How many are the days of thy servant?
> when wilt thou execute judgment on them that persecute me?"*

Have you ever had a day when it seemed everyone you knew had a bad
time and dumped them upon you? I have! It caused me to become so burdened
that I could not concentrate on my study and duty as a pastor. I would say to
myself, sometimes out loud in my office, *"How long do I have to put with this?
When is it going to get better?"* I believe King David had days like that, and he finally spoke to his spirit three times.

> *"Why art thou cast down, O my soul? And why art thou disquieted
> in me? hope thou in God: for I shall yet praise him for the <u>help</u> of
> his countenance." Psalm 42: 5*

"Why art thou cast down, O my soul? And why art thou disquieted within me? hope thou in God for I shall yet praise him, who is the <u>health</u> of my countenance, and my God." Psalm 42: 11

"Why art thou cast down, O my soul? And why art thou disquieted within me? hope thou in God for I shall yet praise him, who is the <u>health</u> of my countenance, and my God." Psalm 43: 15

Read these three scriptures and count to three and read all the scriptures in both Psalms before you blow a fuse and have to repent!

<u>*VERSE EIGHTY-FIVE:*</u> *"The proud have digged pits for me, which are not after thy law."*

Repeat the procedure described in the commentary in verse eighty-four!

<u>*VERSE EIGHTY SIX:*</u> *"All thy commandments are faithful: they persecute me wrongfully; help thou me."*

As born again by the Spirit Christians, we all know that God's commandments are faithful. But there are those who do not know them they persecute those of us who strive to keep them; not in a physical way but in a way that is really insulting to God himself. My prayer for them is this: *"Father they are willfully ignorant of anything regarding their creator, but you still love them. Father open their spirit to the Holy Ghost who will convict them of their sin and help them repent and be born again for they do not know what they are doing to themselves."*

Jesus said: *"Father, forgive them; for they know not what they do."* Luke 23: 34

Stephen stated the following while he was being stoned to death: *"Lord, lay not this sin to their charge."* Acts 7: 60

Should we not have the same type of compassion toward those who persecute us for our faith?

<u>*VERSE EIGHTY-SEVEN:*</u> *"They had almost consumed me upon earth; but I forsook not thy precepts."*

Sometimes we feel tired of trying to witness to people who seem so set in their way of destruction. Let us continue to pray for the lost because unknown to them, they are going to suffer hell fire for all eternity.

"Have I any pleasure at all that the wicked should die? Saith the Lord GOD: and not that he should return from his ways, and live?" Ezekiel 18: 23

Let this statement soak into your soulish area when you become weary of dealing with the ignorant and the wicked people of this world. Unfortunately, there are many in the church who call themselves Christians who are ignorant and wicked!

<u>VERSE EIGHTY-EIGHT</u>: *"Quicken me after thy lovingkindness; so shall I keep the testimony of thy mouth."*

I hate sin, God hates sin, but he loves his creation, especially mankind because they are created in his own image. I believe it sorrows him when someone dies without receiving Jesus Christ as their Savior. But he cannot forsake his judgment for their sin. Think of this and we will have more compassion for the lost: they will suffer for their sins for all eternity IN HELL, not just a few moments of time.

My prayer is: quicken my spirit and revive me to the degree of exercising God's mercy, grace, compassion and pray for the Holy Ghost to open our ears to the inner cry of the lost then allow the Holy Ghost to open the door of witness to enable us to lead them to the cross.

There will be a final judgment called the great white throne judgment where the lost will be judged after we enjoy the 1,000-year reign with Christ.

"Blessed and holy is he that hath part in the first resurrection: on such the second death hath no power, but they shall be priests of God and of Christ, and shall reign with him a thousand years. And when the thousand years are expired, Satan shall be loosed out of his prison, And shall go out to deceive the nations which are in the four quarters of the earth, Gog and Magog, to gather them together to battle: the number of whom is as the sand of the sea. And they went up on the breadth of the earth, and compassed the camp of the saints about, and the beloved city: and fire came down from

God out of heaven, and devoured them. And the devil that deceived them was cast into the lake of fire and brimstone, where the beast and the false prophet are, and shall be tormented day and night for ever and ever. And I saw a great white throne, and him that sat on it, from whose face the earth and the heaven fled away; and there was found no place for them. And I saw the dead, small and great, stand before God; and the books were opened: and another book was opened, which is the book of life: and the dead were judged out of those things which were written in the books, according to their works. And the sea gave up the dead which were in it; and death and hell delivered up the dead which were in them: and they were judged every man according to their works. And death and hell were cast into the lake of fire. This is the second death. And whosoever was not found written the book of life was cast into the lake of fire." Revelation 20: 6-15

UNIT TWELVE:

LAMED
Psalm 119: 89-96

VERSE EIGHTY-NINE: "*Forever, O LORD, thy word is settled in heaven.*"

As I read this verse, I discovered a great source of security knowing that I am following the truth as the Holy Ghost is leading me. Science has tried to explain away many things through analyzation but has failed to prove anything different than what the Word of God has already stated. God has already settled it! I believe it and it is settled not only in Heaven but in my spirit as well.

"Shew me thy ways, O LORD; teach me thy paths. Lead me in thy truth, and teach me: for thou art the God of my salvation; on thee do I wait all the day. Remember, O LORD, thy tender mercies and thy loving kindnesses; for they have been ever of old. Remember not the sins of my youth, nor my transgressions: according to thy mercy remember thou me for thy goodness' sake, O LORD. Good and upright is the LORD: therefore will he teach sinners in the way. The meek will he guide in judgment: and the meek will he teach his way. All the paths of the LORD are mercy and truth unto such as keep his covenant and his testimonies." Psalm 25: 4-10

VERSE NINETY: "*Thy faithfulness is unto all generations: thou hast established the earth, and it abideth.*"

Cultures change with every generation, but God's faithfulness never changes. He offers salvation through the blood of Jesus Christ whereby we are born again by the Spirit. He does not change with man's culture; he is always the same! He established the Earth in its orbit, and it has revolved the same since creation!

My prayer to God is: *"Let me be faithful in returning thanks to you for all you have done in my personal life. Help me through the leading of the Holy Ghost to conform to the image of your Son which is your predestined plan for my life. Amen"*

> *VERSE NINETY-ONE:* *"They continue this day according to thine ordinances: for all are thy servants."*

The Earth, Sun and Moon continue to function as God created them to do. This furnishes us as human beings to have our life furnished with exactly what we need. Their functions demonstrate God's faithful eternal care for humanity and his eternal power!

> *"Behold, bless ye the LORD, all ye servants of the LORD, which by night stand in the house of the LORD. Lift up your hands in the sanctuary, and bless the LORD. The LORD that made heaven and earth bless thee out of Zion." Psalm 134: 1-3*

> *VERSE NINETY-TWO:* *"Unless thy law had been my delights, I should then have perished in mine affliction."*

God's eternal laws establish trust and safety when we love and obey them.

Personally, I would have not survived life to this point without the power contained in the Word. It has brought me through many a storm of doubt and depression because it is not just words printed on a page; the Word is alive, and it lives within my soul. God, you are my refuge and I abide underneath your everlasting arms.

> *"Unless the LORD had been my help, my soul had almost dwelt in silence. When I said, My foot slippeth; thy mercy, O LORD, held me up. In the multitude of my thoughts within me thy comforts delight my soul. Shall the throne of iniquity have fellowship with thee, which frameth mischief by a law? They gather themselves together against the soul of the righteous, and condemn the innocent*

blood. But the LORD is my defense; and my God is the rock of my refuge." Psalm 94: 17-22

<u>*VERSE NINETY-THREE*</u>: *"I will never forget thy precepts: for with them thou hast quickened me."*

Father, your Word is scribed upon my heart and in my mind; in times of pressure, the Holy Ghost brings just the right scriptures to help me overcome! Help me listen more and talk less!

"Wherein in time past ye walked according to the course of this world, according to the prince of the power of the air, the spirit that now worketh in the children of disobedience: Among whom also we all had our conversation in times past in the lusts of our flesh, fulfilling the desires of the flesh and of the mind; and were by nature the children of wrath, even as others. But God, who is rich in mercy, for his great love wherewith he loved us, Even when we were dead in sins, hath quickened us together with Christ, (by grace ye are saved;) And hath raised us up together, and made us sit together in heavenly places in Christ Jesus: That in the ages to come he might shew the exceeding riches of his grace in his kindness toward us through Christ Jesus." Ephesians 2: 2-7

<u>*VERSE NINETY-FOUR*</u>: *"I am thine, save me; for I have sought thy precepts."*

Early in my Christian life when I sought God's precepts, I was looking for more purpose for my life and ministry; my main motive as a born again by the Spirit Christian was to live for Christ. All my early life before becoming born again was to be successful and to be somebody! I wanted riches, comfort and yes, people I loved to be proud of my accomplishments. I was like this for years; even after I was called into the ministry, these things were my motivation. But many years ago now, I found that all the acclimations in my life counted for nothing; they faded away quickly. The joy of the Lord in ministry through the anointing is what has brought me the rewarding acclimation in Christ that all the years I worked myself into the ground to receive. My all in all is in my Father who loves me!

<u>*VERSE NINETY-FIVE:*</u> *"The wicked have waited for me to destroy me: but I will consider thy testimonies."*

I worked for years to support my family in the newspaper industry and was very successful and ministered until 1995. I found myself in the midst of wickedness and went through what the corporations in America call downsizing, etc. In the two years prior to 1995, I was downsized to where I started in my career, a salesman. My salary was cut considerably, but I was granted a commission percentage. God provided me the best area of the city I lived in at the time for prospective customers, and within a month I was making more money than I had made in the management position with fewer headaches. Yes, the wicked tried its best to destroy my faith, but God, through the leadership of the Holy Ghost, did not allow that to happen.

I kept my mind on the victorious testimonies in the Word of God and found more support and revenues that the world had ever offered me without the stress! I love the story of Gideon. Below is just a portion of his story. Read the whole story in the book of Judges chapter 7.

> *"When I blow with a trumpet, I and all that are with me, then blow ye the trumpets also on every side of all the camp, and say, The sword of the LORD, and of Gideon. So Gideon, and the hundred men that were with him, came unto the outside of the camp in the beginning of the middle watch; and they had but newly set the watch: and they blew the trumpets, and brake the pitchers that were in their hands. And the three companies blew the trumpets, and brake the pitchers, and held the lamps in their left hands, and the trumpets in their right hands to blow withal: and they cried, The sword of the LORD, and of Gideon. And they stood every man in his place round about the camp: and all the host ran, and cried, and fled. And the three hundred blew the trumpets, and the LORD set every man's sword against his fellow, even throughout all the host: and the host fled to Beth-shittah in Zererath, and to the border of Abel-meholah, unto Tabbath.'" Judges 7: 18-22*

> <u>*VERSE NINETY-SIX:*</u> *"I have seen an end of all perfection: but thy commandment is exceeding broad."*

I have seen many things that man has proclaimed to be perfect, but when you look closely, you can always find a flaw. There are no flaws in God's workmanship. The flaws we see in our lives are caused by what happened in the garden. Mankind brought on their problems when they fell from the perfection he had provided for them.

> *"The law of the LORD is perfect, converting the soul: the testimony of the LORD is sure, making wise the simple. The statutes of the LORD are right, rejoicing the heart: the commandment of the LORD is pure, enlightening the eyes. The fear of the LORD is clean, enduring for ever: the judgments of the LORD are true and righteous altogether. More to be desired are they than gold, yea, than much fine gold: sweeter also than honey and the honeycomb. Moreover by them is thy servant warned: and in keeping of them there is great reward. Who can under-stand his errors? cleanse thou me from secret faults. Keep back thy servant also from presumptuous sins; let them not have dominion over me: then shall I be up-*

UNIT THIRTEEN:

MEM
Psalm 119: 97-104

VERSE NINETY-SEVEN AND NINETY-EIGHT: *"O how love I thy law! it is my meditation all the day. Thou through thy commandments hast made me wiser than mine enemies: for they are ever with me."*

Many times, when we read the Bible, we read too quickly. We should stroll through the Word as we would a beautiful garden filled with all kinds of blooming plants. Each plant produces unique blossoms filled with aroma for us to enjoy. The Bible is filled with Spirit inspired words and phrases that have special meanings; meanings we can only harvest if we meditate upon them and allow the Holy Ghost to let us read between the lines to find truth!

Then when the accuser begins his attack, we can know the Word and exercise the wisdom God gives us to not even consider the attack. But rejoice that we are overcomers through the faith we receive through meditating upon the Word long enough to know the great power of God is with us!

"The steps of a good man are ordered by the LORD: and he delighteth in his way. Though he fall, he shall not be utterly cast down: for the LORD upholdeth him with his hand. I have been young, and now am old; yet have I not seen the righteous forsaken, nor his seed begging bread. He is ever merciful, and lendeth; and

his seed is blessed. Depart from evil, and do good; and dwell for evermore. For the LORD loveth judgment, and forsaketh not his saints; they are preserved for ever: but the seed of the wicked shall be cut off. The righteous shall inherit the land, and dwell therein forever. The mouth of the righteous speaketh wisdom, and his tongue talketh of judgment. The law of his God is in his heart; none of his steps shall slide. The wicked watcheth the righteous, and seeketh to slay him. The LORD will not leave him in his hand, nor condemn him when he is judged. Wait on the Lord, and keep his way, and he shall exalt thee to inherit the land: when the wicked are cut off, thou shalt see it." Psalm 37: 23-34

<u>VERSE NINETY-NINE</u>: *"I have more understanding than all my teachers: for thy testimonies are my meditation."*

At first glance at this verse, it sounds very egoistic. But when one realizes what the Holy Ghost can teach, one can really have more understanding than all the teaching and preaching heard in a lifetime. We as teachers and preachers are to be led by the Holy Ghost into truth to help people open their individual mind and spirit to receive more truth. That is only accomplished when a student of the Bible will spend time in meditation of the scriptures, not just speed reading the Bible.

Peter left the following words in his second letter, chapter one, verses 15-21:

"Moreover I will endeavour that ye may be able after my decease to have these things always in remembrance. For we have not followed cunningly devised fables, when we made known unto you the power and coming of our Lord Jesus Christ, but were eyewitnesses of his majesty. For he received from God the Father honour and glory, when there came such a voice to him from the excellent glory, This is my beloved Son, in whom I am well pleased. And this voice which came from heaven we heard, when we were with him in the holy mount. We have also a more sure word of prophecy; whereunto ye do well that ye take heed, as unto a light that shineth in a dark place, until the day dawn, and the day star arise in your hearts: Knowing this first; that no prophecy of the scripture is of any private interpretation. For the prophecy came not in old time by the <u>will of man</u>: but holy men of God spake as they were <u>moved by the Holy Ghost</u>."

The Holy Ghost is still speaking truth today. But always remember; the truth will always be verified by what saith the Lord God in the Holy Scriptures. We must have the discernment of spirits while we are meditating on the scriptures; the enemy of our soul knows the Word of God very well and can twist the Scriptures to trip us up as he did with Eve in the Garden of Eden.

VERSE ONE HUNDRED: *"I understand more than the ancients, because I keep thy precepts."*

Once again we must be careful with this statement. It is easy to be deceived into thinking one wiser than someone else in the Scriptures. This leads to pride, and pride leads to a fall. True understanding comes from spiritual meditation that is led by the Holy Ghost, not human interpretation.

We must know and honor the precepts of God to be advanced in our understanding of the Holy Scriptures. It is okay to utilize commentaries, but always remember they are just commentaries and not always fully true. The Holy Ghost is the only identity that can lead one into truth. Obedience to the law of God will do more than any mere human teaching to make a man or woman truly wise.

David spoke the following words when he was delivered out of the hand of the enemy and out of the hand of Saul because he knew God as his fortress, deliverer, shield, salvation, tower, refuge and savior:

"For I have kept the ways of the LORD, and have not wickedly departed from my God. For all his judgments were before me: and as for his statutes, I did not depart from them. I was also upright before him, and have kept myself from mine iniquity. There-fore the Lord hath recompensed me according to my righteousness; according to my cleanness in his eye sight. With the merciful thou wilt shew thyself merciful, and with the upright man thou wilt shew thyself upright." 2 Samuel 22: 22-26

VERSE ONE HUNDRED ONE: *"I have refrained my feet from every evil way, that I might keep thy word."*

When I am enticed to think carnally instead of spiritually, I remember what David stated in Psalm 119: 105 which is in unit fourteen.

We as born again by the Spirit Christians must avoid all the allurements of this world. We are bought with a great price that being, the blood of the Lord Jesus Christ and we must not walk in disobedience of his Word because we love and desire to serve him.

> *"Finally; be ye all of one mind, having compassion one of another, love as brethren, be pitiful, be courteous: Not rendering evil for evil, or railing for railing: but contrariwise blessing; knowing that ye are thereunto called, that ye should inherit a blessing. For he that will love life, and see good days, let him refrain his tongue from evil, and his lips that they speak no guile: Let him eschew evil, and do good; let him seek peace, and ensue it. For the eyes of the Lord are over the righteous, and his ears are open unto their prayers: but the face of the Lord is against them that do evil. And who is he that will harm you, if ye be followers of that which is good?" 1 Peter 3: 8-13*

> <u>*VERSE ONE HUNDRED TWO:*</u> *"I have not departed from thy judgments: for thou hast taught me."*

This does not mean I have never done this, but that a greater part of my life I have done it! The character and aim of my life have been obedience, not disobedience. When I have sinned against his judgments, the Holy Ghost has brought it to my attention, and I have repented. I cannot boast of my own wisdom but in the wisdom that comes from above. Thank God, I have the Holy Ghost to guide me into all truth and convict me when I am wrong.

> *"This then is the message which we have heard of him, and declare unto you, that God is light, and in him is no darkness at all. If we say that we have fellowship with him, and walk in darkness, we lie, and do not the truth: But if we walk in the light, as he is in the light, we have fellowship one with another, and the blood of Jesus Christ his Son cleanseth us from all sin. If we say that we have no sin, we deceive ourselves, and the truth is not in us. If we confess our sins, he is faithful and just to forgive us our sins, and to cleanse us from all unrighteous-ness. If we say that we have not sinned, we make him a liar, and his word is not in us." 1 John 1: 5-10*

> <u>VERSE ONE HUNDRED THREE:</u> *"How sweet are thy words unto my taste! yea, sweeter than honey to my mouth!"*

My wife makes the best pastries, cakes, pies and fruit loaves I have ever tasted. Her pie crust melts in my mouth. It is her fault that I weigh as much as I do; really it is my fault because I have no tolerance when it comes to sweets. But the Word of God has become just as tasty to me as her wonderful desserts. I pray that the Holy Ghost will make me spiritually fat as he leads me into more truth.

> *"The law of the LORD is perfect, converting the soul: the testimony of the LORD is sure, making wise the simple. The statutes of the LORD are right, rejoicing the heart: the commandment of the LORD is pure, enlightening the eyes. The fear of the LORD is clean, enduring forever: the judgments of the LORD are true and righteous altogether. More to be desired are they than gold, yea, that much fine gold: sweeter also than honey and the honeycomb. More-over to them is thy servant warned: and in keeping of them there is great reward. Who can understand his errors? cleanse thou me from secret faults. Keep back thy servant also from presumptuous sins; let them not have dominion over me: then shall I be upright, and I shall be innocent from the great transgression. Let the words of my mouth, and the meditation of my heart, be acceptable in thy sight, O LORD, my strength, and my redeemer." Psalm 19: 7-14*

> <u>*VERSE ONE HUNDRED FOUR:*</u> *"Through thy precepts I get understanding; therefore I hate every false way."*

I am thankful for the guidance of the Holy Ghost as I study, because he gives me true understanding. It is not my human nature to truly understand things. I had problems in school understanding many things; therefore, I was not a straight A student. Plus, because of my unguided ambition to succeed, I got myself into financial problems in my early years and my family suffered, but praise the Lord, he loved me before I was born again by the Spirit and he provided for my family even though it was a struggle. God is so good! I hate that which is false and evil.

> *"The thoughts of the righteous are right: but the counsels of the wicked are deceit. The words of the wicked are to lie in wait for blood: but the mouth of the upright shall deliver them. The wicked*

are overthrown, and are not: but the house of the righteous shall stand. A man shall be commended according to his wisdom: but he that is of a perverse heart shall be despised. He that is despised, and hath a servant, is better than he that honoureth himself, and lacketh bread. A righteous man regardeth the life of his beast: but the tender mercies of the wicked are cruel. He that tilleth his land shall be satisfied with bread: but he that followeth vain persons is void of under-standing. The wicked desireth the net of evil men: but the root of the righteous yieldeth fruit. The wicked is snared by the transgression of his lips: but the just shall come out of trouble. A man shall be satisfied with good by the fruit of his mouth: and the recompence of a man's hands shall be rendered unto him. The way of a fool is right in his own eyes: but he that hearkeneth unto counsel is wise. A fool's wrath is presently known: but a prudent man covereth shame. He that speaketh truth sheweth forth righteousness: but a false witness deceit. There is that speaketh like the piercings of a sword: but the tongue of the wise is health. The lip of truth shall be established for ever: but a lying tongue is but for a moment. Deceit is in the heart of them that imagine evil: but to the counsellers of peace is joy. There shall no evil happen to the just: but the wicked shall be filled with mischief. Lying lips are abomination to the LORD: but they that deal truly are his delight. A prudent man concealeth knowledge: but the heart of fools proclaimeth foolishness. The hand of the diligent shall bear rule: but the slothful shall be under tribute. Heaviness in the heart of man maketh it stoop: but a good word maketh it glad. The righteous is more excellent than his neighbour: but the way of the wicked seduceth them. The slothful man roasteth not that which he took in hunting: but the substance of a diligent man is precious. In the way of righteousness is life; and in the pathway thereof there is no death." Proverbs 12: 5-28

UNIT FOURTEEN:

NUN
Psalm 119: 105-112

<u>*VERSE ONE HUNDRED FIVE:*</u> *"Thy word is a lamp unto my feet, and a light unto my path."*

Since Jesus is the light of the world and he is the Word, he is the illumination we need to walk in this dark, sin-filled world. He and the power of the Holy Ghost he sent to us and dwells in us will guide us in truth where there is no deceit. We will be enabled to not stumble or fall into traps that will lead us into eternal danger. What a wonderful God, our Abba Father, we serve and love. Because we walk in the light as Jesus is in the light, we can be assured to dwell in victory while we walk in a troublesome world.

"Hear me when I call, O God of my righteousness: thou hast enlarged me when I was in distress; have mercy upon me, and hear my prayer. O ye sons of men, how long will ye turn my glory into shame? how long will ye love vanity, and seek after leasing? Selah. But know that the LORD hath set apart him that is godly for himself: the LORD will hear when I call unto him. Stand in awe, and sin not: commune with your own heart upon your bed, and be still. Selah. Offer the sacrifices of righteousness, and put your trust in the LORD. There be many that say, Who will shew us any good? LORD, lift thou up the light of thy countenance upon us. Thou hast put gladness in my heart, more than in the time that their

corn and their wine increased. I will both lay me down in peace, and sleep: for thou, LORD, only makest me dwell in safety." Psalm 4: 1-8

<u>VERSE ONE HUNDRED SIX:</u> *"I have sworn, and I will perform it, that I will keep thy righteous judgments."*

I am careful to keep my portion of the covenant Jesus established on the cross of Calvary.

In general, not being judgmental, there are many people who say they are Christians but in character they closely relate to the world and expect to make Heaven. They confess to *"know and believe"* in Jesus but live like the devil and expect to abide in the Holy of Holies! May I be so bold as to inform the reader of this study that Lucifer and his angels in Heaven that fell with him knowing who Jesus is and they fear and tremble! Should we as born again by the Spirit Christians not do the same and live according to the righteous judgments of our God, our Loving Abba Father!

Let us show more respect and love to our God by worshiping in Spirit and in Truth!

"Servants, be obedient to them that are your masters according to the flesh, with fear and trembling, in singleness of your heart, as unto Christ; Not with eyeservice, as menpleasers; but as the servants of Christ, doing the will of God from the heart; With good will doing service, as to the Lord, and not to men: Knowing that whatsoever good thing any man doeth, the same shall he receive of the Lord, whether he be bond or free." Ephesians 6: 5-8

"Let us draw near with a true heart in full assurance of faith, having our hearts sprinkled from an evil conscience, and our bodies washed with pure water. Let us hold fast the profession of our faith without wavering; (for he is faithful that promised;) And let us consider one another to provoke unto love and to good works: Not forsaking the assembling of ourselves together, as the manner of some is; but exhorting one another: and so much the more, as ye see the day approaching." Hebrews 10: 22-25

<u>VERSE ONE HUNDRED SEVEN:</u> *"I am afflicted very much: quicken me, O LORD, according unto thy word."*

Many times our Lord allows us to be afflicted to get our attention. I personally have been afflicted financially, physically, and spiritually in times past when I was so consumed with myself. Believe me; God knows how to get our attention!

James points out something very interesting in chapter five, verse 13: he states, *"Is any among you afflicted? Let him pray."* It doesn't take a genius to figure this statement out! We can be in any number afflictions, but we are not to ask anyone to pray for us; we are to pray for ourselves. Why? God wants to hear from us and speak words of wisdom to us! We as ministers get so busy doing church work we forget to really spend time with our Father in prayer. So what does he do? What any loving Father would do, he gets our attention!

We need to stop by the throne room often and allow the Holy Ghost to quicken us to converse with the one who has called us into ministry. Sure, we know how to do things, but God knows a better way. Why not trust him and allow him to give us wisdom and anointing through the power of the Holy Ghost when we preach *HIS* word!

Read the account of Daniel's life in chapter four, five and six. Daniel knew the things that were coming against him, but he continued to pray as he always did because he enjoyed fellowship with God.

> *"Now when Daniel knew that the writing was signed, he went into his house; and his windows being open in his chamber toward Jeru-salem, he kneeled upon his knees three times a day, and prayed, and gave thanks before his God, as he did aforetime."* Daniel 6: 10

Daniel was a man of prayer; he did not allow the coming affliction to deter him. What an example for a minister to follow instead of calling an emergency board meeting.

> *VERSE ONE HUNDRED EIGHT:* *"Accept, I beseech thee, the freewill offerings of my mouth, O LORD, and teach me thy judgments."*

Note the words *"freewill offerings"*. I am not talking about money. Let us offer ourselves to God freely as living sacrifices. Let our speech be full of anointing and wisdom as willingly offer ourselves to be taught at the feet of Jesus the Christ!

<u>*VERSE ONE HUNDRED NINE:*</u> *"My soul is continually in my hand: yet do I not forget thy law."*

I must say I have a problem when people proclaim eternal security and do not study and keep the commandments of Jesus. God gives us a free will and our eternal security is to be taken seriously.

It is my firm conviction when we are genuinely born again by the Spirit we are indeed freed from our past sins. But does that mean we can live a life of sin the rest of our life and still go to Heaven when we die? I think not! Or as Paul states in Romans 6: 1, 2, God forbid!

I do not hold to the idea of working our way to Heaven. However, I do believe we must maintain a healthy lifestyle after salvation. To me salvation through the precious blood of Jesus Christ demands fidelity. Our accuser is always on the lookout to trip us up. We are victorious against him when we study and obey the Word of God. This helps us meditate upon the Word instead of conforming to the ways of the world. Let us work on conforming to the image of Jesus the Christ as stated in Romans 8: 29.

"Then said Jesus to those Jews which believed on him, If ye continue in my word, then are ye my disciples indeed; And ye shall know the truth, and the truth shall make you free." John 8: 31-32

"If ye continue in the faith grounded and settled, and be not moved away from the hope of the gospel, which ye have heard, and which was preached to every creature which is under heaven." Colossians 1: 23

"For if God spared not the natural branches, take heed lest he also spare not thee. Behold therefore the goodness and severity of God: on them which fell, severity; but toward thee, goodness, if thou continue in his goodness: otherwise thou also shalt be cut off. And they also, if they abide not still in unbelief, shall be graffed in: for God is able to graff them in again. For if thou wert cut out of the olive tree which is wild by nature, and wert graffed contrary to nature into a good olive tree: how much more shall these, which be the natural branches, be graffed into their own olive tree? For I would not, brethren, that ye should be ignorant of this mystery, lest ye should be wise in your own conceits; that blindness in part is happened to Israel, until the fulness of the Gentiles be come in. And so all Israel shall be saved: as it is written, There shall come out of Sion the Deliverer, and shall turn away ungodliness from Jacob: For this is my covenant unto them, when I shall take away their sins. As concerning the gospel, they are enemies for your sakes: but as touching the election, they are beloved for the fathers' sakes. For the gifts and calling of God are without repentance; For as ye in times past have not believed God, yet have now obtained mercy through their unbelief: Even so have these also now not believed, that through your mercy they also may obtain mercy. For God hath concluded them all in unbelief, that he might have mercy upon all.

O the depth of the riches both of the wisdom and knowledge of God! How unsearchable are his judgments, and his ways past finding out! For who hath known the mind of the Lord? or who hath been his counsellor? Or who hath first given to him, and it shall be recompensed unto him again? For of him, and through him, and to him, are all things: to whom be glory forever. Amen." Romans 11: 21-36

Jesus himself established the covenant upon the cross by shedding his blood to suffering physical death; how dare we trample his blood under our feet by living a sinful lifestyle after we have been born again by the Spirit of God.

"Fight the good fight of faith, lay hold on eternal life, whereunto thou art also called, and hast professed a good profession before many witnesses." 1 Timothy 6:12

<u>VERSE ONE HUNDRED TEN</u>: *"The wicked have laid a snare for me: yet I erred not from thy precepts."*

I don't know if I have ever met a born again by the Spirit Christian who has never had a snare laid for them. But I have met many who have overcome the snare by trusting in the Words of Jesus!

"Heaven and earth shall pass away: but my words shall not pass away. And take heed to yourselves, lest at any time your hearts be overcharged with surfeiting, and drunkenness, and cares of this life, and so that day come upon you unawares. For as a snare shall it come on all them that dwell on the face of the whole earth. Watch ye therefore, and pray always, that ye may be accounted worthy to escape all these things that shall come to pass, and to stand before the Son of man." Luke 21: 33-36

<u>*VERSE ONE HUNDRED ELEVEN*</u>: *"Thy testimonies have I taken as an heritage forever: for they are the rejoicing of my heart."*

When we accept the heritage of Christ Jesus and enjoy its awards, we will always find ourselves rejoicing in his Word for it is truth! The Holy

Ghost leads everyone who loves peace into a joy that is their strength in times of testing.

> *"Peace I leave with you, my peace I give unto you: not as the world giveth, give I unto you. Let not your heart be troubled, neither let it be afraid." John 14: 27*

> *"These things I have spoken unto you, that in me ye might have peace. In the world ye shall have tribulation: but be of good cheer; I have overcome the world." John 16: 33*

> <u>*VERSE ONE HUNDRED TWELVE:*</u> *"I have inclined mine heart to perform thy statutes alway, even unto the end."*

When we accept the love of God and become born again by the Spirit believers, we have become a new creature. However, we must commit our mind to learning the Scriptures to overcome the former human mind.

> *"This I say therefore, and testify in the Lord, that ye henceforth walk not as other Gentiles walk, in the vanity of their mind, Having the understanding darkened, being alienated from the life of God through the ignorance that is in them, because of the blindness of their heart: Who being past feeling have given themselves over unto lasciviousness, to work all uncleanness with greediness. But ye have not so learned Christ; If so be that ye have heard him, and have been taught by him, as the truth is in Jesus: That ye put off concerning the former conversation the old man, which is corrupt according to the deceitful lusts; And be renewed in the spirit of your mind; And that ye put on the new man, which after God is created in righteousness and true holiness. Wherefore putting away lying, speak every man truth with his neighbour: for we are members one of another. Be ye angry, and sin not: let not the sun go down upon your wrath: Neither give place to the devil." Ephesians 4: 17-27*

UNIT FIFTEEN:

SAMECH
Psalm 119: 113-120

VERSE ONE HUNDRED THIRTEEN: *"I hate vain thoughts: but thy law do I love."*

I have battled vain thoughts in my dreams of my mistakes in judgment many times in the past. I wake up in the night and have to shake myself into reality. The things that I could have done different, wrong career discussions, etc. cannot be redone; they are past. I have started praising the Lord when I go to bed a long time ago by lifting my hands in surrender and asking the Lord to rebuke the enemy for me, and it is working!

The more of God's Word we can store in our memory cells, the more rest we can receive when we sleep.

"Thou wilt keep him in perfect peace, whose name is stayed on thee: because he trusteth in thee. Trust you in the Lord forever; for in the Lord Jehovah is everlasting strength." Isaiah 26: 3, 4

"Hear me when I call, O God of my righteousness: thou hast enlarged me when I was in distress; have mercy upon me, and hear my prayer. O ye sons of men, how long will ye turn my glory into shame? How long will ye love vanity, and seek after leasing? Selah. But know that the LORD hath set apart him that is godly for himself: the LORD will hear when I call unto him. Stand in awe, and

sin not: commune with your own heart upon your bed, and be still. Selah. Offer the sacrifices of righteousness, and put your trust in the LORD. There be many that say, who will shew us any good? LORD, lift thou up the light of thy countenance upon us. Thou hast put gladness in my heart, more than in the time that their corn and their wine increased. I will both lay me down in peace, and sleep: for thou, LORD, only makest me dwell in safety." Psalm 4: 1-8

<u>VERSE ONE HUNDRED FOURTEEN:</u> *"Thou art my hiding place and my shield: I hope in thy word."*

One of Abraham Lincoln's troop stated, *"We trust, Sir, that God is on our side."* Lincoln replied, *"It is more important to know that we are on God's side."*

As great as our nation's military is, it is foolish to think they can keep us from harm. We are still a nation whose slogan is *"In God we trust"*! When our nation's leaders lean on the arm of flesh, we are not safe; we are only safe when we lean upon the one who created both good and evil and are still in control of both. We must continue to have faith in God; he never changes. Jesus makes the statement in Matthew 28: 18: *"all power is given unto me in heaven and in earth."* I still believe that truth and my hope remains in his Word!

"Blessed is he whose transgression is forgiven, whose sin is covered. Blessed is the man unto whom the LORD imputeth not iniquity, and in whose spirit there is no guile. When I kept silence, my bones waxed old through my roaring all the day long. For day and night thy hand was heavy upon me: my moisture is turned into the drought of summer. Selah. I acknow-ledged my sin unto thee, and mine iniquity have I not hid. I said, I will confess my transgressions unto the LORD; and thou forgavest the iniquity of my sin. Selah. For this shall every one that is godly pray unto thee in a time when thou mayest be found: surely in the floods of great waters they shall not come nigh unto him. Thou art my hiding place; thou shalt pre-serve me from trouble; thou shalt compass me about with songs of deliverance. Selah. I will instruct thee and teach thee in the way which thou shalt go: I will guide thee with mine eye. Be ye not as the horse, or as the mule, which have no understanding: whose mouth must be held in with bit and bridle, lest they come near unto

*thee. Many sorrows shall be to the wicked: but he that trusteth in
the LORD, mercy shall compass him about. Be glad in the LORD,
and rejoice, ye righteous: and shout for joy, all ye that are upright
in heart." Psalm 32: 1-11*

<u>*VERSE ONE HUNDRED FIFTEEN:*</u> *"Depart from me, ye
evildoers: for I will keep the commandments of my God."*

The only time we should be in the presence of evildoers is when the Holy
Ghost opens the door to be a witness to them. Otherwise it is wisdom to stay
out of their territory particularly if one is a new Christian and does not know
the Word; they may be allured to partake of their foolish, sinful lifestyles.

We must keep our hearts fixed upon what saith the LORD GOD in a society who justifies conforming to worldly allurements.

> *"Be ye not unequally yoked together with unbelievers: for what fel-
> lowship hath righteousness with unrighteousness? and what com-
> munion hath light with darkness? And what concord hath Christ
> with Belial? or what part hath he that believeth with an infidel?
> And what agreement hath the temple of God with idols? for ye are
> the temple of the living God; as God hath said, I will dwell in them,
> and walk in them; and I will be their God, and they shall be my
> people. Wherefore come out from among them, and be ye separate,
> saith the Lord, and touch not the unclean thing; and I will receive
> you, And will be a Father unto you, and ye shall be my sons and
> daughters, saith the Lord Almighty." 2 Corinthians 6: 14-18*

<u>*VERSE ONE HUNDRED SIXTEEN:*</u> *"Uphold me according unto
thy word, that I may live: and let me not be ashamed of my hope."*

If we will call upon the help of the Holy Ghost, he will sustain us in our
trials and temptations and help us rejoice in hope instead of being ashamed.

Religion has no power to uphold our hope, but true Christianity will deliver us from the evil of this world and even cause us to blush at the things
happening around us and turn from them.

> *"Forasmuch then as the children are partakers of flesh and blood,
> he also himself likewise took part of the same; that through death*

he might destroy him that had the power of death, that is, the devil; And deliver them who through fear of death were all their lifetime subject to bondage. For verily he took not on him the nature of angels; but he took on him the seed of Abraham. Wherefore in all things it behoved him to be made like unto his brethren, that he might be a merciful and faithful high priest in things pertaining to God, to make reconciliation for the sins of the people. For in that he himself hath suffered being tempted, he is able to succour them that are tempted." Hebrews 2: 14-18

"Therefore being justified by faith, we have peace with God through our Lord Jesus Christ: By whom also we have access by faith into this grace wherein we stand, and rejoice in hope of the glory of God. And not only so, but we glory in tribulations also: knowing that tribulation worketh patience; And patience, experience; and experience, hope: And hope maketh not ashamed; because the love of God is shed abroad in our hearts by the Holy Ghost which is given unto us.For when we were yet without strength, in due time Christ died for the ungodly. For scarcely for a righteous man will one die: yet peradventure for a good man some would even dare to die. But God commendeth his love toward us, in that, while we were yet sinners, Christ died for us. Much more then, being now justified by his blood, we shall be saved from wrath through him." Romans 5: 1-9

<u>VERSE ONE HUNDRED SEVENTEEN:</u> *"Hold thou me up, and I shall be safe: and I will have respect unto thy statutes continually."*

Spurgeon said the following of himself: *"I must confess that I have a daily fighting of my better self against the old self, the newborn nature against the old nature, which will, If it can, still keep its hold upon me."* It is said Spurgeon had a problem with a bad temper. I am sure this was one of the things he battled with!

We are still captured in our old bodies and must contend with them through the power of the Holy Ghost if we are serious about our Christianity. God's power can keep us *if* we will keep our mind upon him and his Holy Word. When we feel ourselves wandering, pull out the holy road map and find the right path to follow. This is the fight of faith!

"Rejoice evermore. Pray without ceasing. In everything give thanks: for this is the will of God in Christ Jesus concerning you. Quench not the Spirit. Despise not prophesying's. Prove all things; hold fast that which is good. Abstain from all appearance of evil. And the very God of peace sanctify you wholly; and I pray God your whole spirit and soul and body be preserved blameless unto the coming of our Lord Jesus Christ. Faithful is he that calleth you, who also will do it." 1 Thessalonians 5:16-24

<u>*VERSE ONE HUNDRED EIGHTTEEN*</u>: *"Thou hast trodden down all them that err from thy statutes: for their deceit is falsehood."*

We must be careful of self-righteousness in the process of this particular scripture and look to the truth. We know there are people who interpreted the scriptures to their own benefit. However, they are the creation of God, and we must help them overcome the false deceit. The Word of God does not need to be defended through human arguments but obeyed! When one does not accept the truth, then leave them to their falsehood.

The secret of fulfilling this scripture is to know the truth and be a steadfast follower of that truth!

"Now when the congregation was broken up, many of the Jews and religious proselytes followed Paul and Barnabas: who, speaking to them, persuaded them to continue in the grace of God. And the next sabbath day came almost the whole city together to hear the word of God. But when the Jews saw the multitudes, they were filled with envy, and spake against those things which were spoken by Paul, contradicting and blaspheming. Then Paul and Barnabas waxed bold, and said, It was necessary that the word of God should first have been spoken to you: but seeing ye put it from you, and judge yourselves unworthy of everlasting life, lo, we turn to the Gentiles. For so hath the Lord commanded us, saying, I have set thee to be a light of the Gentiles, that thou shouldest be for salvation unto the ends of the earth. And when the Gentiles heard this, they were glad, and glorified the word of the Lord: and as many as were ordained to eternal life believed. And the word of the Lord was published throughout all the region. But the Jews stirred up the devout and honourable women, and the chief men of the city, and raised

persecution against Paul and Barnabas, and expelled them out of their coasts. But they shook off the dust of their feet against them, and came unto Iconium. And the disciples were filled with joy, and with the Holy Ghost." Acts 13:43-52

<u>**VERSE ONE HUNDRED NINETEEN:**</u> *"Thou puttest away all the wicked of the earth like dross: therefore I love thy testimonies."*

The major problem, in my opinion, is that the 21st century church is conforming to worldly sounds and activity. The Holy Scriptures state that we are not to remove the landmarks; God's landmarks were established for a reason. That reason being to remind us of what God has done and will continue to do if we will be obedient followers of truth!

We are not to change our testimonies, nor our worship to fit the culture of the world. In the transition, much of the Godly reverence is lost and the flesh is justified instead of Jesus Christ being glorified!

"Why, seeing times are not hidden from the Almighty, do they that know him not see his days Some remove the landmarks; they violently take away flocks, and feed thereof They drive away the ass of the fatherless, they take the widow's ox for a pledge They turn the needy out of the way: the poor of the earth hide themselves together. Behold, as wild asses in the desert, go they forth to their work; rising betimes for a prey: the wilderness yieldeth food for them and for their children. They reap every one his corn in the field: and they gather the vintage of the wicked. They cause the naked to lodge without clothing, that they have no covering in the cold. They are wet with the showers of the mountains, and embrace the rock for want of a shelter. They pluck the father-less from the breast, and take a pledge of the poor. They cause him to go naked without clothing, and they take away the sheaf from the hungry; Which make oil within their walls, and tread their winepresses, and suffer thirst. Men groan from out of the city, and the soul of the wounded crieth out: yet God layeth not folly to them. They are of those that rebel against the light; they know not the ways thereof, nor abide in the paths thereof. The murderer rising with the light killeth the poor and needy, and in the night is as a thief. The eye also of the adulterer waiteth for the twilight, saying, No eye shall see me: and dis-

guiseth his face In the dark they dig through houses, which they had marked for themselves in the daytime: they know not the light. For the morning is to them even as the shadow of death: if one know them, they are in the terrors of the shadow of death. He is swift as the waters; their portion is cursed in the earth: he beholdeth not the way of the vineyards. Drought and heat consume the snow waters: so doth the grave those which have sinned. The womb shall forget him; the worm shall feed sweetly on him; he shall be no more remember-ed; and wickedness shall be broken as a tree. He evil en-treateth the barren that beareth not: and doeth not good to the widow. He draweth also the mighty with his power: he riseth up, and no man is sure of life. Though it be given him to be in safety, whereon he resteth; yet his eyes are upon their ways. They are ex-alted for a little while, but are gone and brought low; they are taken out of the way as all other, and cut off as the tops of the ears of corn. And if it be not so now, who will make me a liar, and make my speech nothing worth?" Job 24: 1-25

<u>*VERSE ONE HUNDRED TWENTY*</u>: *"My flesh trembleth for fear of thee; and I am afraid of thy judgments."*

I fear and tremble in the presence of God's holiness; he is the Alpha and Omega in the bodily presence of Jesus Christ our Lord. He holds my life in the palm of his hand. This fear is a holy fear of respect and honor for the one who came to Earth in physical form, endured all temptation victoriously, con-quered death, Hell, and the grave and is now seated at the right hand of the father. He is gracious and just, and he is coming for those who are love and are looking for his appearing.

He deserves to be strictly obeyed in our physical and spiritual life. He paid the price for our salvation and left us a covenant to honor.

"Thus saith the LORD, The heaven is my throne, and the earth is my footstool: where is the house that ye build unto me? and where is the place of my rest? For all those things hath mine hand made, and those things have been, saith the LORD: but to this man will I look, even to him that is poor and of a contrite spirit, and trem-bleth at my word." Isaiah 66: 1-2

"…Moses was learned in all the wisdom of the Egyptians, and was

mighty in words and in deeds. And when he was full forty years old, it came into his heart to visit his brethren the children of Israel. And seeing one of them suffer wrong, he defended him, and avenged him that was oppressed, and smote the Egyptian: For he supposed his brethren would have understood how that God by his hand would deliver them: but they understood not. And the next day he shewed himself unto them as they strove, and would have set them at one again, saying, Sirs, ye are brethren; why do ye wrong one to another? But he that did his neighbour wrong thrust him away, saying, Who made thee a ruler and a judge over us? Wilt thou kill me, as thou diddest the Egyptian yesterday? Then fled Moses at this saying, and was a stranger in the land of Madian, where he begat two sons. And when forty years were expired, there appeared to him in the wilderness of Mount Sina and angel of the Lord in a flame of fire in a bush when Moses saw it he nwondered at the sight: and as he drew near to behold it, the voice of the Lord came unto him, Saying, I am the God of thy fathers, the God of Abraham, and the God of Isaac, and the God of Jacob. Then Moses trembled, and durst not behold. Then said the Lord to him, Put off thy shoes from thy feet: for the place where thou standest is holy ground." Acts 7: 22-33

Everybody is going to stand in judgment either at the Judgment Seat of Christ, or the Great White Throne Judgment! 2 Corinthians 5: 10; Revelation 20: 11-15.

UNIT SIXTEEN:

AIN
Psalm 119: 121-128

<u>*VERSE ONE HUNDRED TWENTY-ONE:*</u> *"I have done judgment and justice: leave me not to mine oppressors."*

In response to the first portion of this scripture, I can only say I am only righteous through the Blood of Jesus, not of my own judgments and justice. It is by the work of the mercy and grace of God that I am a born again by the Spirit Christian.

In response to the second portion of this Scripture, as far as I know I am not oppressed by anyone, certainly not by the enemy of my soul as I ask the Lord daily to rebuke him.

> *"Thus saith the LORD, In an acceptable time have I heard thee, and in a day of salvation have I helped thee: and I will preserve thee, and give thee for a covenant of the people, to establish the earth, to cause to inherit the desolate heritages; That thou mayest say to the prisoners, Go forth; to them that are in darkness, Shew yourselves. They shall feed in the ways, and their pastures shall be in all high places. They shall not hunger nor thirst; neither shall the heat nor sun smite them: for he that hath mercy on them shall lead them, even by the springs of water shall he guide them. And I will make all my mountains a way, and my highways shall be exalted. Behold, these shall come from far: and, lo, these from the*

north and from the west; and these from the land of Sinim. Sing, O heavens; and be joyful, O earth; and break forth into singing, O mountains: for the LORD hath comforted his people, and will have mercy upon his afflicted." Isaiah 49: 8-13

<u>VERSE ONE HUNDRED TWENTY TWO:</u> *"Be surety for thy servant for good: let not the proud oppress me."*

Jesus Christ is my High Priest who gives me safe passage on this Earth and is providing good in my life as long as I walk according to the covenant he established on Calvary.

As far as the proud being oppression to me, the proud will fall and fail if they do not repent. My prayer is this: *"Hide me behind the cross which will keep me humble in spirit and rebuke the spoiler from my life."*

When I become perplexed in study, I love to read Proverbs 29: 23-27:

"A man's pride shall bring him low: but honour shall uphold the humble in spirit. Whoso is partner with a thief hateth his own soul: he heareth cursing, and bewrayeth it not. The fear of man bringeth a snare: but whoso putteth his trust in the LORD shall be safe. Many seek the ruler's favour; but every man's judgment cometh from the LORD. An unjust man is an abomination to the just: and he that is upright in the way is abomination to the wicked."

<u>VERSE ONE HUNDRED TWENTY-THREE:</u> *"Mine eyes fail for thy salvation, and for the word of thy righteousness."*

If we will all be honest, there are times when we sit down to study the Word, even though we know we are truly born again by the Spirit, our natural understanding fails us. It is at this point we must stop our study and ask the Holy Ghost to renew our spirit through the righteousness of our Lord Jesus Christ. We must remember there are nuggets of truth sown in the Word that can only by mined through the leading of the Holy Ghost!

When I am studying and I run into something I don't understand, I read Zechariah 4: 1-14, then listen for the still small voice of instruction via the Holy Ghost.

I believe we honor God by asking questions when we cannot comprehend the meaning of things we come to in our study of the Word.

<u>*VERSE ONE HUNDRED TWENTY-FOUR:*</u> *"Deal with thy servant according unto thy mercy, and teach me thy statutes."*

When we come to the throne room and stand before our High Priest [Hebrews 4: 14-16], we do it in faith depending upon his intersession; then God's mercy deals with us as a teacher in the classroom would deal with honest questions concerning a lesson he or she cannot understand.

> *"Blessed be the Lord God of Israel; for he hath visited and redeemed his people, And hath his holy prophets, which have been since the world began: That we should be saved from our enemies, and from the hand of all that hate us; To perform the mercy promised to our fathers, and to remember his holy covenant; The oath which he sware to our father Abraham, That he would grant unto us, that we being delivered out of the hand of our enemies might serve him without fear, In holiness and righteousness before him, all the days of our life. And thou, child, shalt be called the prophet of the Highest: for thou shalt go before the face of the Lord to prepare his ways; To give knowledge of salvation unto his people by the remission of their sins, Through the tender mercy of our God; whereby the dayspring from on high hath visited us, To give light to them that sit in darkness and in the shadow of death, to guide our feet into the way of peace." Luke 1: 68-79*

> <u>*VERSE ONE HUNDRED TWENTY-FIVE:*</u> *"I am thy servant; give me understanding, that I may know thy testimonies."*

If we are to prosper in God's Kingdom Work, let us always have the servitude attitude. When we become proud and arrogant, God cannot use us in the way that will be profitable. We must understand that he respects us when we approach him with a humble and contrite spirit.

> *OUR PRAYER SHOULD BE: "Since I am your servant, instruct me in the knowledge of your will through the leading of the Holy Ghost as I desire to obey you; show me what will be acceptable obedience; what is required in order to be acceptable in service. Amen." I BELIEVE THIS IS A PRAYER OF A PERSON WHO SINCERELY DESIRES TO OBEY GOD.*

> <u>*VERSE ONE HUNDRED TWENTY-SIX:*</u> *"It is time for thee, LORD, to work: for they have made void thy law."*

I believe we are at the point in our American churches where the Lord has been left out of the plan. We have so many books written by various authors that give instruction for building a successful church that the membership is confused. It is time for the Holy Ghost to fall fresh upon our church leaders to humbly fall before God and seek his face in the 21st century. After all, the church belongs to Jesus. Let us as preachers of the gospel make way for him to walk up and down the aisles of the church and love his people.

> *"Which of you shall have a friend, and shall go unto him at midnight, and say unto him, Friend, lend me three loaves; For a friend of mine in his journey is come to me, and I have nothing to set before him? And he from within shall answer and say, Trouble me not: the door is now shut, and my children are with me in bed; I cannot rise and give thee. I say unto you, Though he will not rise and give him, because he is his friend, yet because of his importunity he will rise and give him as many as he needeth. And I say unto you, Ask, and it shall be given you; seek, and ye shall find; knock, and it shall be opened unto you. For every one that asketh receiveth; and he that seeketh findeth; and to him that knocketh it shall be opened. If a son shall ask bread of any of you that is a father, will he give him a stone? or if he ask a fish, will he for a fish give him a serpent? Or if he shall ask an egg, will he offer him a scorpion? If ye then, being evil, know how to give good gifts unto your children: How much more shall your heavenly Father give the Holy Spirit to them that ask him?" Luke 11: 5-13*

> <u>*VERSE ONE HUNDRED TWENTY-SEVEN AND TWENTY-EIGHT*</u>: *"Therefore I love thy commandments above gold; yea, above fine gold. Therefore I esteem all thy precepts concerning all things to be right; and I hate every false way."*

In our world's economy, gold has reached a great price. Why are not the commandments of God increasing in value? People are hording gold coins now because they expect the price to increase more. Is it not true if we would have the same desire for the Word of God, it too would increase in value to the human soul?

Where is the church's focus today? Is it truly obeying God's Word or is it only a false selfish love clothed in pretend love for God's will to see people truly born again by the Spirit? This all sounds very severe, but just look around and see what is happening in the church world. It is a numbers game instead of Godly, obedient worship. The enemy has sown many tares in many of our churches in America.

We must do what Jesus told the church at Ephesus: *"Remember therefore from whence thou art fallen, and repent, and do the first works; or else I will come unto thee quickly, and will remove thy candlestick out of his place, except thou repent."* Revelation 2: 4

Our first work is found in Matthew 22: 37-40!

> *"Thou shalt love the Lord thy God with all thy heart, and with all thy soul, and with all thy mind. This is the first and great commandment. And the second is like unto it, Thou shalt love thy neighbour as thyself. On these two commandments hang all the law and the prophets."*

Then we can truly say:

> *"Therefore I love thy commandments above gold; yea, above fine gold. Therefore I esteem all thy precepts concerning all things to be right; and I hate every false way."*

UNIT SEVENTEEN:

PE
Psalm 119: 129-136

VERSE ONE HUNDRED TWENTY-NINE: "*Thy testimonies are wonderful: therefore doth my soul keep them.*"

There is an old hymn that we used to sing many years ago that describe how wonderful the testimonies of the Holy Word mean to me: the song is entitled "Wonderful Words of Life" written by P. P. Bliss; copy right by Stamps Baxter music BMI; all rights controlled by The Benson Company Inc. Nashville, TN.

The lyrics are:

VERSE ONE:

Sing them over again to me, Wonderful words of Life;
let me more of their beauty see,
Wonderful words of Life.
Words of life and beauty, teach me faith and duty:

VERSE TWO:

Christ the blessed One gives to all, Wonderful words of Life;
Sinner list to the loving call,
Wonderful words of Life.
All so freely given, working us to heaven:

Sweetly echo the gospel call, Wonderful words of Life;
Offer pardon and peace to all,
Wonderful words of Life,
Jesus only Saviour, Sanctify forever:

CHORUS:

Beautiful words, wonderful words of Life, Wonderful words of life.

My mind and spirit stands in awe of the wisdom contained in the Word; a wisdom that can only be understood as the Holy Ghost leads me through the verses of truth and the truth is manifested in my spirit which quickens my eternal soul into victorious living.

"Verily, verily, I say unto you, Except ye eat the flesh of the Son of man, and drink his blood, ye have no life in you. Whoso eateth my flesh, and drinketh my blood, hath eternal life; and I will raise him up at the last day. For my flesh is meat indeed, and my blood is drink indeed; He that eateth my flesh, and drinketh my blood, dwelleth in me, and I in him. As the living Father hath sent me, and I live by the Father: so he that eateth me, even he shall live by me. This is that bread which came down from heaven: not as your fathers did eat manna, and are dead: he that eateth of this bread shall live forever. These things said he in the synagogue, as he taught in Capernaum. Many therefore of his disciples, when they had heard this, said, This is an hard saying; who can hear it? When Jesus knew in himself that his disciples murmured at it, he said unto them, Doth this offend you? What and if ye shall see the Son of man ascend up where he was before? It is the spirit that quicke-neth; the flesh profiteth nothing: the words that I speak unto you, they are spirit, and they are life. But there are some of you that be-lieve not. For Jesus knew from the beginning who they were that believed not, and who should betray him. And he said, Therefore said I unto you, that no man can come unto me, except it were given unto him of my Father. From that time many of his disciples went back, and walked no more with him. Then said Jesus unto the

twelve, Will ye also go away? <u>Then Simon Peter answered him,</u>
<u>Lord, to whom shall we go? thou hast the words of eternal life. And</u>
<u>we believe and are sure that thou art that Christ, the Son of the</u>
<u>living God.</u>" John 6: 53-69

This is a very wonderful portion of Scripture. When our spiritual person consumes the Word of God, we are actually consuming Jesus' flesh and blood. This is what gives us Spirit and life which leads us to total commitment as born again by the Spirit Christians. His name is called *"THE WORD OF GOD"!* Revelation 19: 13

<u>*VERSE ONE HUNDRED THIRTY:*</u> *"The entrance of thy words giveth light; it giveth understanding unto the simple."*

When we open our mind and spirit to the leading of the Holy Ghost in our study of the Word, it is like walking into a dark room and turning on a bright light. We begin a journey of loving commitment to our Lord, and begin to turn into a vessel of honor to our Father in Heaven. Then the Holy Ghost begins to open opportunities for us to share eternal life to whosoever will accept the truth of the Word.

The Word used in this verse does not mean people who have limited understanding; it means anyone who will open the door of the heart, mind and spirit to the leading of leadership of the Holy Ghost as he leads one into more truth!

"Behold, I stand at the door, and knock: if any man hear my voice, and open the door, I will come in to him, and will sup with him, and he with me. To him that overcometh will I grant to sit with me in my throne, even as I also overcame, and am set down with my Father in his throne." Revelation 3: 20-21

<u>*VERSE ONE HUNDRED THIRTY-ONE:*</u> *"I opened my mouth, and panted: for I longed for thy commandments."*

When we get serious about learning the Scriptures, our heart will increase the blood flow to our brain which causes us to intensely desire to learn more about the Trinity and how it flows from Genesis 1 through Revelation 22: 21.

It is an exciting adventure to study the Scriptures; we will have difficulty understanding some of the Scriptures; that is one of the reasons Jesus prayed the father to send the Holy Ghost to each and every born again by the Spirit Christian. He is our tour guide through the scriptures; he knows all the meanings!

"As the hart panteth after the water brooks, so panteth my soul after thee, O God. My soul thirsteth for God, for the living God: when shall I come and appear before God? My tears have been my meat day and night, while they continually say unto me; Where is thy God? When I remember these things, I pour out my soul in me: for I had gone with the multitude, I went with them to the house of God, with the voice of joy and praise, with a multitude that kept holyday." Psalm 42: 1-4

VERSE ONE HUNDRED THIRTY-TWO: "Look thou upon me, and be merciful unto me, as thou usest to do unto those that love thy name."

Sometimes we as born again by the Spirit Christians grow lax in our love for God, and we have to do what Jesus told the church at Ephesus as we previously stated earlier.

"Unto the angel of the church of Ephesus write; These things saith he that holdeth the seven stars in his right hand, who walketh in the midst of the seven golden candlesticks I know thy works, and thy labour, and thy patience, and how thou canst not bear them which are evil: and thou hast tried them which say they are apostles, and are not, and hast found them liars: And hast borne, and hast patience, and for my name's sake hast laboured, and hast not fainted. Nevertheless I have somewhat against thee, because thou hast left thy first love. Remember therefore from whence thou art fallen, and repent, and do the first works; or else I will come unto thee quickly, and will remove thy candlestick out of his place, except thou repent. But this thou hast, that thou hatest the deeds of the Nicolaitans, which I also hate. He that hath an ear, let him hear what the Spirit saith unto the churches; To him that overcometh will I give to eat of the tree of life, which is in the midst of the paradise of God." Revelation 2: 1-7

God responds to us in a wonderful way when we express our love for his only begotten Son, Jesus, who was sacrificed for our sins. Also, we are welcomed into the throne room because of Jesus who is our scepter of righteousness.

<u>*VERSE ONE HUNDRED THIRTY-THREE*</u>: *"Order my steps in thy word: and let not any iniquity have dominion over me."*

We are not robots; we are created human beings, created by God with a free will; we can go and come in this world any way we choose to. However, for our steps to be ordered by God, and in order for iniquity to not have dominion over us, we must confess our sins, repent and allow God to help us change into what he created us to become through the guidance of the Holy Ghost.

I believe the reasoning of this particular scripture is to will ourselves to commit to God and his ways, not our own. I know there are times we cry out to God to help us in our walk. However, I believe the more of the Word we can learn, our conduct will conform to the image that Jesus set forth while he walked the Earth in human flesh. The devil is our accuser; he is very good at what he does. But he cannot touch us if we will stay in Christ and allow our Lord to rebuke him.

"There is therefore now no condemnation to them which are in Christ Jesus, who walk not after the flesh, but after the Spirit. For the law of the Spirit of life in Christ Jesus hath made me free from the law of sin and death. For what the law could not do, in that it was weak through the flesh, God sending his own Son in the likeness of sinful flesh, and for sin, condemned sin in the flesh: That the righteousness of the law might be fulfilled in us, who walk not after the flesh, but after the Spirit. For they that are after the flesh do mind the things of the flesh; but they that are after the Spirit the things of the Spirit; For to be carnally minded is death; but to be spiritually minded is life and peace. Because the carnal mind is enmity against God: for it is not subject to the law of God, neither indeed can be. So then they that are in the flesh cannot please God. But ye are not in the flesh, but in the Spirit, if so be that the Spirit of God dwell in you. Now if any man have not the Spirit of Christ,

he is none of his. And if Christ be in you, the body is dead because of sin; but the Spirit is life because of righteousness. But if the Spirit of him that raised up Jesus from the dead dwell in you, he that raised up Christ from the dead shall also quicken your mortal bodies by his Spirit that dwelleth in you. Therefore, brethren, we are debtors, not to the flesh, to live after the flesh. For if ye live after the flesh, ye shall die: but if ye through the Spirit do mortify the deeds of the body, ye shall live. For as many as are led by the Spirit of God, they are the sons of God. For ye have not received the spirit of bondage again to fear; but ye have received the Spirit of adoption, whereby we cry, Abba, Father. The Spirit itself beareth witness with our spirit, that we are the children of God: And if children, then heirs; heirs of God, together." Romans 8: 1-17

"For whom he did foreknow, he also did predestinate to be conformed to the image of his Son, that he might be the firstborn among many brethren. Moreover whom he did predestinate, them he also called: and whom he called, them he also justified: and whom he justified, them he also glorified. What shall we then say to these things? If God be for us, who can be against us? He that spared not his own Son, but delivered him up for us all, how shall he not with him also freely give us all things? Who shall lay anything to the charge of God's elect? It is God that justifieth." Romans 8: 29-33

If we want to live a life of overcoming victory, we must make it a practice to feed our mind and spirit with the BREAD OF LIFE, which is the Word and the Word is Jesus. We are to ignore the accuser and not by bringing a railing accusation against him; our Lord will do that is we ask him to do so!

"Beloved, when I gave all diligence to write unto you of the common salvation, it was needful for me to write unto you, and exhort you that ye should earnestly contend for the faith which was once delivered unto the saints. For there are certain men crept in unawares, who were before of old ordained to this condemnation, ungodly men, turning the grace of our God into lasciviousness, and denying the only Lord God, and our Lord Jesus Christ. I will therefore put you in remembrance, though ye once knew this, how that the Lord, having saved the people out of the land of Egypt, afterward destroyed them that believed not. And the angels which kept not their first estate, but left their own habitation, he hath reserved in everlasting chains under

darkness unto the judgment of the great day. Even as Sodom and Go-morrha, and the cities about them in like manner, giving themselves over to fornication, and going after strange flesh, are set forth for an example, suffering the vengeance of eternal fire. Likewise also these filthy dreamers defile the flesh, despise dominion, and speak evil of dignities. Yet Michael the archangel, when contending with the devil he disputed about the body of Moses, durst not bring against him a railing accusation, but said, The Lord rebuke thee." Jude 3-9

<u>*VERSE ONE HUNDRED THIRTY-FOUR:*</u> *"Deliver me from the oppression of man: so will I keep thy precepts."*

Man-made doctrines have put more people in bondage than any rotten sin they may have committed. If one would allow the Holy Ghost to guide them into all truth, which is studying and comparing scripture to scripture from Genesis 1 through Revelation 22: 21, they would find themselves in line with the covenant Jesus established on the cross. There are some things we may not truly understand in the process, but be assured the truth the Holy Ghost leads into the truth that will set us free from the bondage of the enemy and mankind.

"Verily, verily, I say unto you, Whosoever committeth sin is the servant of sin. And the servant abideth not in the house for ever: but the Son abideth ever. If the Son therefore shall make you free, ye shall be free indeed." John 8: 34-36

<u>*VERSE ONE HUNDRED THIRTY-FIVE:*</u> *"Make thy face to shine upon thy servant; and teach me thy statutes."*

In response to this scripture, I love the words the apostle Paul wrote to the Philippian church. He exhorted them to fulfill his joy he had in them. I believe a direct message from Jesus to you and I would sound similar as we walk and have our being upon this Earth. Let me—let us—be faithful pilgrims together for the glory of God. Let our countenance be bright and full of God's glory. I believe the day of our home going is soon. At my age, I know mine is. Come soon, my Jesus, my Savior. I'm ready!

"Let this mind be in you, which was also in Christ Jesus: Who, being in the form of God, thought it not robbery to be equal with

God: But made himself of no reputation, and took upon him the form of a servant, and was made in the likeness of men: And being found in fashion as a man, he humbled himself, and became obedient unto death, even the death of The cross. Wherefore God also hath highly exalted him, and given him a name which is above every name: That at the name of Jesus every knee should bow, of things in heaven, and things in earth, and things under the earth; And that every tongue should confess that Jesus Christ is Lord, to the glory of God the Father. Wherefore, my beloved, as ye have always obeyed, not as in my presence only, but now much more in my absence, work out your own salvation with fear and trembling. For it is God which worketh in you both to will and to do of his good pleasure. Do all things without murmurings and disputings: That ye may be blameless and harmless, the sons of God, without rebuke, in the midst of a crooked and perverse nation, among whom ye shine as lights in the world; Holding forth the word of life; that I may rejoice in the day of Christ, that I have not run in vain, neither laboured in vain." Philippians 2: 5-16

<u>*VERSE ONE HUNDRED THIRTY-SIX:*</u> *"Rivers of waters run down mine eyes, because they keep not thy law."*

I am sure we all have family members and friends who are lost or maybe lukewarm who bring sorrow to our hearts. Let us not be faint hearted but continue praying diligently that the Holy Ghost will deal with their hearts and they will choose Jesus as their personal savior before the end of their journey on this Earth.

As you read the following, consider the groaning and sorrowful statement Jesus uttered as he overlooked all the sins of Jerusalem:

"O Jerusalem, Jerusalem, thou that killest the prophets, and stonest them which are sent unto thee, how often would I have gathered thy children together, even as a hen gathereth her chickens under her wings, and ye would not!" Matthew 23: 37 and Luke 13: 34

"They that sow in tears shall reap in joy. He that goeth forth and weepeth, bearing precious seed, shall doubtless come again with rejoicing, bringing his sheaves with him." Psalm 126: 5-6

UNIT EIGHTTEEN:

TZADDI
Psalm 119: 137-144

<u>*VERSE ONE HUNDRED THIRTY-SEVEN*</u>: *"Righteous art thou, O LORD, and upright are thy judgments."*

There is no doubt in my mind that the eternal God is righteous and all together righteous in judgment, mercy and grace. He is absolutely my only God! He is equal and fair to all his creation; we are the one who make life unequal. It was a sad day when Israel requested a king to be over them instead of God. Man's legislation is not equal in today's world.

Many of the judges and politicians of today are the same as those in Israel were; they take bribes and show favoritism to people of power and become rich. We are still living in sad days. But one of these days it will change when the Lord of Lords comes to take his bride from the face of this Earth.

"And it came to pass, when Samuel was old, that he made his sons judges over Israel. Now the name of his firstborn was Joel; and the name of his second, Abiah: they were judges in Beersheba. And his sons walked not in his ways, but turned aside after lucre, and took bribes, and perverted judgment. Then all the elders of Israel gathered themselves together, and came to Samuel unto Ramah, And said unto him, Behold, thou art old, and thy sons walk not in thy ways: now make us a king to judge us like all the nations. But the

<u>VERSE ONE HUNDRED THIRTY-EIGHT</u>: *"Thy testimonies that thou hast commanded are righteous and very faithful."*

What amazes me: God is still equal to those who have put their trust in the Lord Jesus Christ by becoming born again by the Spirit. He is fair to all. He blesses the faithful who dare to obey his commandments even though in much of the world, and it is starting to be true in our own nation, it is against the laws mankind has instituted to speak of the damnation of those who transgress against the Holy Word of God Almighty. The world calls it a hate message, but it is not; it is a help message to save the persons involved in ungodly activity and abomination to be saved from God's wrath.

be my disciples. As the Father hath loved me, so have I loved you: continue ye in my love. If ye keep my commandments, ye shall abide in my love; even as I have kept my Father's commandments, and abide in his love. These things have I spoken unto you, that my joy might remain in you, and that your joy might be full. This is my commandment, That ye love one another, as I have loved you. Greater love hath no man than this; that a man lay down his life for his friends; Ye are my friends, if ye do whatsoever I command you." John 15: 1-14

Every born against the Spirit Christian becomes a branch of the vine, who is Jesus. We are to grow in faith then share the gospel with anyone and everyone who will listen.

<u>*VERSE ONE HUNDRED THIRTY-NINE:*</u> *"My zeal hath consumed me, because mine enemies have forgotten thy words."*

I refuse to allow this to happen to me! I will not be negative and become discouraged because people will not remember God's Word and apply it to their life and lifestyle. It is my goal, even at my age, to continue preaching and teaching the truth of the Word: *"he that sinneth will die and go to Hell."* But I will preach and teach it in the Spirit of the aanointed love of God. Why? Unfortunately, in our Christian nation, there are those who are ignorant concerning the ways of God because they have only heard his name mentioned in profanity. They do not know God loves them; they need to hear that rather than preaching messages of condemnation. I still believe even the worst sinner alive is looking for an answer to get out of the hole they are in. Unfortunately, they are searching in the wrong avenues. Let us who are preachers and teachers be zealous to preach the truth that there is a Hell to shun, but let us do it properly as to not cause confusion like what happened in the Corinthian church.

"Follow after charity, and desire spiritual gifts, but rather that ye may prophesy. For he that speaketh in an unknown tongue speaketh not unto men, but unto God: for no man under-standeth him; howbeit in the spirit he speaketh mysteries. But he that prophesieth speaketh unto men to edification, and exhortation, and comfort. He that speaketh in an unknown tongue edifieth himself; but he that prophesieth edifieth the church. I would that ye all spake with

tongues, but rather that ye prophesied: for greater is he that proph-esieth than he that speaketh with tongues, except he interpret, that the church may receive edifying. Now, brethren, if I come unto you speaking with tongues, what shall I profit you, except I shall speak to you either by revelation, or by knowledge, or by prophesying, or by doctrine? And even things without life giving sound, whether pipe or harp, except they give a distinction in the sounds, how shall it be known what is piped or harped? For if the trumpet give an un-certain sound, who shall prepare himself to the battle? So like-wise ye, except ye utter by the tongue words easy to be understood, how shall it be known what is spoken? for ye shall speak into the air. There are, it may be, so many kinds of voices in the world, and none of them is without signification. Therefore if I know not the meaning of the voice, I shall be unto him that speaketh a barbarian, and he that speaketh shall be a barbarian unto me. Even so ye, for-asmuch as ye are zealous of spiritual gifts, seek that ye may excel to the edifying of the church." 1 Corinthians 14: 1-12

<u>*VERSE ONE HUNDRED AND FORTY:*</u> *"Thy word is very pure: therefore thy servant loveth it."*

The company that makes Ivory soap claims it is 99% pure and it rinses clean. There are no perfumes or deodorant chemicals in it to remain on one's skin. That is the kind of Gospel we need to be preached from the pulpits in the 21st century, a pure clean Gospel that will refresh the souls of the listener and remove the dirt from the sinner. The Word of God is 100% pure; why not preach it in purity as the Holy Ghost us anoints us?

"Behold, what manner of love the Father hath bestowed upon us, that we should be called the sons of God: therefore the world kno-weth us not, because it knew him not. Beloved, now are we the sons of God, and it doth not yet appear what we shall be: but we know that, when he shall appear, we shall be like him; for we shall see him as he is. And every man that hath this hope in him purifieth himself, even as he is pure." 1 John 3: 1-3

<u>*VERSE ONE HUNDRED AND FORTY ONE:*</u> *"I am small and despised: yet do not I forget thy precepts."*

One may only have the opportunity to preach and teach a small congregation; of a truth, in every congregation big or small, one can't make everyone happy, but one still has the obligation to preach the truth in love. We must not be ashamed of preaching the Gospel, but we should feel honored to represent the kingdom of God wherever we may be serving him.

David was despised by his brothers because he was just a small young man; they accused him of being prideful, but he knew God and his power because he communed with him while tending the sheep in the wilderness.

"And David said to Saul, Let no man's heart fail because of him; thy servant will go and fight with this Philistine. And Saul said to David, Thou art not able to go against this Philistine to fight with him: for thou art but a youth, and he a man of war from his youth. And David said unto Saul, Thy servant kept his father's sheep, and there came a lion, and a bear, and took a lamb out of the flock: And I went out after him, and smote him, and delivered it out of his mouth: and when he arose against me, I caught him by his beard, and smote him, and slew him. Thy servant slew both the lion and the bear: and this uncircumcised Philistine shall be as one of them, seeing he hath defied the armies of the living God. David said moreover, The LORD that delivered me out of the paw of the lion, and out of the paw of the bear, he will deliver me out of the hand of this Philistine. And Saul said unto David, Go, and the LORD be with thee. And Saul armed David with his armour, and he put an helmet of brass upon his head; also he armed him with a coat of mail. And David girded his sword upon his armour, and he assayed to go; for he had not proved it. And David said unto Saul, I cannot go with these; for I have not proved them. And David put them off him. And he took his staff in his hand, and chose him five smooth stones out of the brook, and put them in a shepherd's bag which he had, even in a script; and his sling was in his hand: and he drew near to the Philistine. And the Philistine came on and drew near unto David; and the man that bare the shield went before him. And when the Philistine looked about, and saw David, he disdained him: for he was but a youth, and ruddy, and of a fair countenance. And the Philistine said unto David, Am I a dog, that thou comest to me with staves? And the Philistine cursed David by his gods. And the Philistine said to David, Come to me, and I will give thy flesh unto the fowls of the air, and to the beasts of the field. Then

said David to the Philistine, Thou comest to me with a sword, and with a spear, and with a shield: but I come to thee in the name of the LORD of hosts, the God of the armies of Israel, whom thou hast defied. This day will the LORD deliver thee into mine hand; and I will smite thee; and I will give the carcases of the host of the Philistines this day unto the fowls of the air, and to the wild beasts of the earth; that all the earth may know that there is a God in Israel. And all this assembly shall know that the LORD saveth not with sword and spear: for the battle is the Lord's, and he will give you into our hands. And it came to pass, when the Philistine arose, and came and drew nigh to meet David, that David hasted, and ran toward the army to meet the Philistine. And David put his hand in his bag, and took thence a stone, and slang it, and smote the Philistine in his forehead, that the stone sunk into his forehead; and he fell upon his face to the earth. So David prevailed over the Philistine with a sling and with a stone, and smote the Philistine, and slew him; but there was no sword in the hand of David. Therefore David ran, and stood upon the Philistine, and took his sword, and drew it out of the sheath thereof, and slew him, and cut off his head therewith. And when the Philistines saw their champion was dead, they fled." 1 Samuel 17:32-51

Let each of us have the fellowship with God as David did and take courage in the life we are living in the 21st century!

VERSE ONE HUNDRED AND FORTY-TWO: *"Thy righteousness is an everlasting righteousness, and thy law is the truth."*

Governments change, customs change, opinions change, people change and the world changes, but God himself never changes, so it is with his law. That law is founded on eternal truth and can never change.

We must understand the law of God is the expression of all truth.

"For I am the LORD, I change not; therefore ye sons of Jacob are not consumed." Malachi 3:6

"Think not that I am come to destroy the law, or the prophets: I am not come to destroy, but to fulfil. For verily I say unto you, Till heaven and earth pass, one jot or one tittle shall in no wise pass

from the law, till all be fulfilled. Whosoever therefore shall break one of these least commandments, and shall teach men so, he shall be called the least in the kingdom of heaven: but whosoever shall do and teach them the same shall be called great in the kingdom of heaven." Matthew 5: 17-19

<u>*VERSE ONE HUNDRED AND FORTY-THREE:*</u> *"Trouble and anguish have taken hold on me: yet thy commandments are my delights."*

During our span of life here on Earth, anguish, troubles and afflictions may come upon us from time to time, but if we are on that narrow path and are headed for the straight gate, we will not be a failure.

When I finally let Jesus into my life, I still struggled with troubles and afflictions, but I knew the Word of God was my anchor that held me in a sure place.

"The name of the LORD is a strong tower: the righteous runneth into it, and is safe." Proverbs 18:10

"Oh that men would praise the LORD for his goodness, and for his wonderful works to the children of men! And let them sacrifice the sacrifices of thanksgiving, and declare his works with rejoicing. They that go down to the sea in ships, that do business in great waters; These see the works of the LORD, and his wonders in the deep. For he commandeth, and raiseth the stormy wind, which lifteth up the waves thereof. They mount up to the heaven, they go down again to the depths: their soul is melted because of trouble. They reel to and fro, and stagger like a drunken man, and are at their wits' end. Then they cry unto the LORD in their trouble, and he bringeth them out of their distresses. He maketh the storm a calm, so that the waves thereof are still. Then are they glad because they be quiet; so he bringeth them unto their desired haven." Psalm 107: 21-30

"And the same day, when the even was come, he saith unto them, Let us pass over unto the other side. And when they had sent away the multitude, they took him even as he was in the ship. And there were also with him other little ships. And there arose a great storm

of wind, and the waves beat into the ship, so that it was now full. And he was in the hinder part of the ship, asleep on a pillow: and they awake him, and say unto him, Master, carest thou not that we perish? And he arose, and rebuked the wind, and said unto the sea, Peace, be still. And the wind ceased, and there was a great calm. And he said unto them, Why are ye so fearful? how is it that ye have no faith? And they feared exceedingly, and said one to another, What manner of man is this, that even the wind and the sea obey him?" Mark 4: 35-41

If we have fear, anguish, troubles and afflictions in our life, let the master of the entire universe speak to our storms.

"All power is given unto me in heaven and in earth." Matthew 28: 18

<u>*VERSE ONE HUNDRED AND FORTY-FOUR:*</u> *"The right-eousness of thy testimonies is everlasting: give me understanding, and I shall live."*

Wow! What a statement of faith. Whenever we consider and believe what Jesus stated in Matthew 28: 18, we can be assured that his righteousness is eternal. This means if we trust him with our soul and our existence here on Earth, we shall live a life of victory no matter the circumstances. I have heard the follow statement made of many Christian people who have this kind of trust: *"They really lived the life!"* They did indeed, and so can we if we be full of faith!

"But without faith it is impossible to please him: for he that cometh to God must believe that he is and that he is a rewarder of them that diligently seek him." Hebrews 11: 6

UNIT NINETEEN:

KOPH
Psalm 119: 145-152

VERSE ONE HUNDRED FORTY-FIVE: *"I cried with my whole heart; hear me, O LORD: I will keep thy statutes."*

When we come to God in prayer, we must open up our entire heart. He will not respond to a double-minded person because they are unstable in all their ways. I have been guilty in my prayers in approaching God with plan a, b, because the truth of the matter is I did not have faith in what I was requesting from God. God knows our heart and request before we ask; he also knows our motives. He is not impressed when we come with half-hearted requests or promises. If we come to him in truth and a heart that is open to his judgment, he will answer. We must be prepared; sometimes the answer is no and sometimes it is yes because he knows our future and knows what is best for us. He will, however, give us wisdom at our request!

"My brethren, count it all joy when ye fall into divers temptations; Knowing this, that the trying of your faith worketh patience. But let patience have her perfect work, that ye may be perfect and entire, wanting nothing. If any of you lack wisdom, let him ask of God, that giveth to all men liberally, and upbraideth not; and it shall be given him. But let him ask in faith, nothing wavering. For he that wavereth is like a wave of the sea driven with the wind and tossed.

For let not that man think that he shall receive any thing of the Lord. A double minded man is unstable in all his ways." James 1: 2-8

<u>VERSE ONE HUNDRED FORTY-SIX</u>: *"I cried unto thee; save me, and I shall keep thy testimonies."*

There have been many times I have cried out to God when I was in trouble spiritually and physically. Sometimes he would hear and answer quickly, and sometimes he would let me stew in my troubles for a while, but he always has been gracious and kind to me.

Human beings are anxious to promise God they will do this or that, if God will hear their cry. But many forget their promise when they are raised up from the verge of destruction and restored to health and prosperity. Many even forget to thank him!

"And it came to pass, as he went to Jerusalem that he passed through the midst of Samaria and Galilee. And as he entered into a certain village, there met him ten men that were lepers, which stood afar off: And they lifted up their voices, and said, Jesus, Master, have mercy on us. And when he saw them, he said unto them, Go shew yourselves unto the priests. And it came to pass, that, as they went, they were cleansed. And one of them, when he saw that he was healed, turned back, and with a loud voice glorified God, And fell down on his face at his feet, giving him thanks: and he was a Samaritan. And Jesus answering said, Were there not ten cleansed? but where are the nine? There are not found that re-turned to give glory to God, save this stranger. And he said unto him, Arise, go thy way: thy faith hath made thee whole." Luke 17: 11-19

<u>*VERSE ONE HUNDRED FORTY-SEVEN*</u>: *"I prevented the dawning of the morning, and cried: I hoped in thy word."*

In the years when I pastored and held a full-time job, I would get up at 4:30 in the morning and spend time before the Lord and seek his guidance for the messages to teach on Wednesday night, Sunday morning and Sunday night. Those were very special times for me.

However, it is not the time of day that is important: it is the time we can find a quiet place where we find hope and consolation. My favorite time now is late in the evening right before I retire.

> *"For he that will love life, and see good days, let him refrain his tongue from evil, and his lips that they speak no guile: Let him eschew evil, and do good; let him seek peace, and ensue it. For the eyes of the Lord are over the righteous, and his ears are open unto their prayers: but the face of the Lord is against them that do evil. And who is he that will harm you, if ye be followers of that which is good?" 1 Peter 3:10-13*

<u>VERSE ONE HUNDRED FORTY-EIGHT</u>: "Mine eyes prevent the night watches that I might meditate in thy word."

As I just said, I prefer the late evening for study and prayer. For years I would have loved to sleep late in the morning. Now that I am retired, I can do so. The Lord has been so good to me, and I give him praise as I meditate study and pray at night.

> *"The LORD is the portion of mine inheritance and of my cup: thou maintainest my lot. The lines are fallen unto me in pleasant places; yea, I have a goodly heritage. I will bless the LORD, who hath given me counsel: my reins also instruct me in the night seasons. I have set the LORD always before me: because he is at my right hand, I shall not be moved. Therefore my heart is glad, and my glory rejoiceth: my flesh also shall rest in hope." Psalm 16: 5-9*

<u>VERSE ONE HUNDRED FORTY-NINE:</u> "Hear my voice according unto thy lovingkindness: O LORD, quicken me according to thy judgment."

It is amazing to me that God hears my voice as there are billions of people on this Earth and probably innumerable people crying out to him in prayer at one time, yet he hears each one of us. I guess it should not be hard to understand; after all, he is God! That means we can know he hears us and will answer our prayers according to his will. His will is the rule of true judgment filled with great promises.

"I love the LORD, because he hath heard my voice and my supplications. Because he hath inclined his ear unto me, therefore will I call upon him as long as I live. The sorrows of death compassed me, and the pains of hell gat hold upon me: I found trouble and sorrow. Then called I upon the name of the LORD; O LORD, I beseech thee, deliver my soul. Gracious is the LORD, and righteous; yea, our God is merciful. The LORD preserveth the simple: I was brought low, and he helped me. Return unto thy rest, O my soul; for the LORD hath dealt bountifully with thee; For thou hast delivered my soul from death, mine eyes from tears, and my feet from falling. I will walk before the LORD in the land of the living. I believed, therefore have I spoken: I was greatly afflicted: I said in my haste, All men are liars. What shall I render unto the LORD for all his benefits toward me? I will take the cup of salvation, and call upon the name of the Lord." Psalm 116: 1-13

<u>*VERSE ONE HUNDRED FIFTY*</u>*: "They draw nigh that follow after mischief: they are far from thy law."*

I am sorry to say that many of our churches have members that are involved in sin and sowing seeds of discord. They are not only harming young Christians, but they are bringing damnation upon themselves.

"These six things doth the LORD hate: yea, seven are an abomination unto him: A proud look, a lying tongue, and hands that shed innocent blood, An heart that deviseth wicked imaginations, feet that be swift in running to mischief, A false witness that speaketh lies, and he that soweth discord among brethren." Proverbs 6: 16-19

<u>*VERSE ONE HUNDRED FIFTY-ONE*</u>*: "Thou art near, O LORD; and all thy commandments are truth."*

When I am awake or asleep, I know my Lord is near, so I do not fear. His commandments are wonderful lines of truth that guide me through my day and give me rest in the night.

This being true, let us consider our walk and conversation here on Earth.

"Let your conversation be without covetousness; and be content with such things as ye have: for he hath said, I will never leave thee, nor forsake thee. So that we may boldly say, The Lord is my helper, and I will not fear what man shall do unto me." He-brews 13: 5, 6

"O Lord, thou hast searched me, and known me. Thou knowest my downstitting and mine uprising, thou unnderstandest my thought afar off. Thou compassest my path and my lying down, and art acquainted with all my ways. For there is not a word in my tongue, but, lo, O LORD, thou knowest it altogether. Thou hast beset me behind and before, and laid thine hand upon me. Such knowledge is too wonderful for me; it is high, I cannot attain unto it. Whither shall I go from thy Spirit? or whither shall I flee from thy presence? If I ascend up into heaven, thou art there: if I make my bed in hell, behold, thou art there. If I take the wings of the morning, and dwell in the uttermost parts of the sea; Even there shall thy hand lead me, and thy right hand shall hold me. If I say, Surely the darkness shall cover me; even the night shall be light about me. Yea, the darkness hideth not from thee; but the night shineth as the day: the darkness and the light are both alike to thee. For thou hast possessed my reins: thou hast covered me in my mother's womb. I will praise thee; for I am fearfully and wonderfully made: marvellous are thy works; and that my soul knoweth right well. My substance was not hid from thee, when I was made in secret, and curiously wrought in the lowest parts of the earth. Thine eyes did see my substance, yet being unperfect; and in thy book all my members were written, which in continuance were fashioned, when as yet there was none of them. How precious also are thy thoughts unto me, O God! How great is the sum of them! If I should count them, they are more in number than the sand: when I awake, I am still with thee. Surely thou wilt slay the wicked, O God: depart from me therefore, ye bloody men. For they speak against thee wickedly, and thine enemies take thy name in vain. Do not I hate them, O LORD, that hate thee? and am not I grieved with those that rise up against thee? I hate them with perfect hatred: I count them mine enemies. Search me, O God, and know my heart: try me, and know my thoughts: And see if there be any wicked way in me, and lead me in the way everlasting." Psalm 139: 1-24

<u>*VERSE ONE HUNDRED FIFTY-TWO:*</u> *"Concerning thy testimonies, I have known of old that thou hast founded them forever."*

Holy Father, when I read your testimonies over and over, they bring me peace and joy. They give foundation to my life and a surety of your creative power.

My prayer is this:

"Lord Jesus, continue your intercession for my soul and grant me the privilege to serve you up to the day of my death here on earth or the rapture of the church whichever comes first. I long to see your power working in and through my life daily in order to keep me refreshed in the spirit and receive ministry so I may minister to others who need you so desperately. Amen!"

"Create in me a clean heart, O God; and renew a right spirit within me. Cast me not away from thy presence; and take not thy holy spirit from me. Restore unto me the joy of thy salvation; and uphold me with thy free spirit. Then will I teach transgressors thy ways; and sinners shall be converted unto thee. Deliver me from blood guiltiness, O God, thou God of my salvation: and my tongue shall sing aloud of thy righteousness. O Lord, open thou my lips; and my mouth shall shew forth thy praise." Psalm 51: 10-15

UNIT TWENTY:

RESH
Psalm 119: 153-160

<u>VERSE ONE HUNDRED FIFTY-THREE:</u> "Consider mine affliction, and deliver me: for I do not forget thy law."

As I read this scripture, I am not entirely acquainted with what my affliction is at this point in my life. I know this: I will not forget THE WORD because it is my life. I feel there is so much more that I can do for the kingdom, but my body tells me that I must not place myself in a position of too much stress. So all I know to do at this point is to be obedient, submissive and patient and serve you as you open opportunities to me that will bless and praise your holy name.

"I will extol thee, my God, O king; and I will bless thy name for ever and ever. Every day will I bless thee; and I will praise thy name for ever and ever. Great is the LORD, and greatly to be praised; and his greatness is unsearchable. One generation shall praise thy works to another, and shall declare thy mighty acts. I will speak of the glorious honour of thy majesty, and of thy wondrous works. And men shall speak of the might of thy terrible acts: and I will declare thy greatness. They shall abundantly utter the memory of thy great goodness, and shall sing of thy righteousness. The LORD is gracious, and full of compassion; slow to anger, and of great mercy. The LORD is good to all: and his tender mercies are over all his works.

All thy works shall praise thee, O LORD; and thy saints shall bless thee. They shall speak of the glory of thy kingdom, and talk of thy power; To make known to the sons of men his mighty acts, and the glorious majesty of his kingdom. Thy kingdom is an everlasting kingdom, and thy dominion endureth throughout all generations. The LORD upholdeth all that fall, and raiseth up all those that be bowed down. The eyes of all wait upon thee; and thou givest them their meat in due season. Thou openest thine hand, and satisfiest the desire of every living thing. The LORD is righteous in all his ways, and holy in all his works. The LORD is nigh unto all them that call upon him, to all that call upon him in truth. He will fulfil the desire of them that fear him: he also will hear their cry, and will save them. The LORD preserveth all them that love him: but all the wicked will he destroy. My mouth shall speak the praise of the LORD: and let all flesh bless his holy name for ever and ever." *Psalm 145: 1-21*

<u>VERSE ONE HUNDRED FIFTY-FOUR</u>: *"Plead my cause, and deliver me: quicken me according to thy word."*

Once again, I am in a place of desire, wanting to do more, but restricted because of my health. One part of me wants to say "Take me home if you are not going to totally heal me"; another part is crying out for you to quicken me according to your purpose while I am here. Please give me more victory or bring me home!

"God be merciful unto us, and bless us; and cause his face to shine upon us; Selah. That thy way may be known upon earth, thy saving health among all nations. Let the people praise thee, O God; let all the people praise thee. O let the nations be glad and sing for joy: for thou shalt judge the people righteously, and govern the nations upon earth. Selah. Let the people praise thee, O God; let all the people praise thee. Then shall the earth yield her increase; and God, even our own God, shall bless us. God shall bless us; and all the ends of the earth shall fear him." *Psalm 67: 1-7*

<u>*VERSE ONE HUNDRED FIFTY-FIVE:*</u> *"Salvation is far from the wicked: for they seek not thy statutes."*

Within the last few years, it has been more difficult to convince people of the world that they need Jesus Christ as their Savior and Lord. We have many that will walk the aisle many Sundays out of conviction, but the seed of the Word seems to be falling upon unfertile soil. In a few weeks, they begin to fall out of church ,and before you know it, they are back in their old lifestyle. This scripture is right on track for the twenty-first century.

In my opinion, the reason for this is people confess with the mouth, but they do not believe in their heart and become born again by the Spirit and move into spiritual growth.

Also, in my opinion, we make it too easy to confess that one really believes. They shake the pastor's hand, become baptized and some really mean it at the time, but they really have not become born again by the Spirit until they become humble and contrite in spirit.

Until they are truly sorry in their sins, they are very far from being safe, or from having a prospect of salvation; they are constantly going farther and farther off, making their salvation less probable, not going toward Heaven, but from it. Distraction is very near to them, and they are constantly making it nearer and nearer. To become born again by the Spirit, they must change their course altogether, and go *toward* salvation and not from it.

"There was a man of the Pharisees, named Nicodemus, a ruler of the Jews: The same came to Jesus by night, and said unto him, Rabbi, we know that thou art a teacher come from God: for no man can do these miracles that thou doest, except God be with him. Jesus answered and said unto him, Verily, verily, I say unto thee, Except a man be born again, he cannot see the kingdom of God. Nicodemus saith unto him, How can a man be born when he is old? can he enter the second time into his mother's womb, and be born? Jesus answered, Verily, verily, I say unto thee, Except a man be born of water and of the Spirit, he cannot enter into the kingdom of God. That which is born of the flesh is flesh; and that which is born of the Spirit is spirit. Marvel not that I said unto thee, Ye must be born again." John 3: 1-7

We cannot lay the blame completely upon the sinner; we who have been born again by the Spirit must be a beacon for them to see the light in us which is Jesus Christ himself!

VERSE ONE HUNDRED FIFTY-SIX: "Great are thy tender mercies, O LORD: quicken me according to thy judgments."

We must remember the mercy of God is great and his grace is abundant. There is a song I sang many times that constantly reminds me of God's tender mercies. The lyrics are listed below. Let us be quickened by the Holy Ghost and be merciful to those who do not know the way heaven. You may be surprised to hear this, but our nation is really not a Christian nation; it is full of religions, but the true born again by the Spirit Christian is a rarity in many of our states.

Mercy, unmerited favor;
Unworthy to be called one of his own
I'm able to face a tomorrow without fear
And every day can be another day like this.
Grateful; so glad he saved me,
Wealthy; because I'm of a child of the king:
May I rest in silent darkness long before I make him grieve,
If I should fail to praise the one who set me free.

CHORUS:

Mercy is the reason I can have a hope today.
While the world goes on in darkness
Desperately to find their way;
Not that I deserve the sacrifice he made on Calvary
But he gave his life for whosoever will and that means me.

BRIDGE:

I was lost, but now I'm found, was blind but now I see,
He left his throne for an old rugged cross
To save someone like me,

REPEAT CHORUS:

"Mercy is the Reason"; produced by David Patello, Hearatwrite Music Texarkana, Arkansas; www.devidpatillo

Psalm 25: 1-11 offers a great prayer that is helpful to the born again by the Spirit Christian as well as the sinner:

> *"Unto thee, O LORD, do I lift up my soul. O my God, I trust in thee: let me not be ashamed, let not mine enemies triumph over me. Yea, let none that wait on thee be ashamed: let them be ashamed which transgress without cause. Shew me thy ways, O LORD; teach me thy paths. Lead me in thy truth, and teach me: for thou art the God of my salvation; on thee do I wait all the day. Remember, O LORD, thy tender mercies and thy lovingkindnesses; for they have been ever of old. Remember not the sins of my youth, nor my transgressions: according to thy mercy remember thou me for thy goodness' sake, O LORD. Good and upright is the LORD: therefore will he teach sinners in the way. The meek will he guide in judgment: and the meek will he teach his way. All the paths of the LORD are mercy and truth unto such as keep his covenant and his testimonies. For thy name's sake, O LORD, pardon mine iniquity; for it is great."*

> *VERSE ONE HUNDRED FIFTY-SEVEN: "Many are my persecutors and mine enemies; yet do I not decline from thy testimonies."*

The only persecution and enemies I may have only come from those who do not understand the truths of the Word of God; unfortunately, there are those who are professing confessing Christians that fit into that category.

In order for me to maintain my Christian integrity, I must not strike back; however, I do not fellowship with such people unless the Holy Ghost opens the door to do so. Then it is to be handled with merciful Word-filled exhortation.

> *"Take heed, brethren, lest there be in any of you an evil heart of unbelief, in departing from the living God. But exhort one another daily, while it is called To day; lest any of you be hardened through*

<u>VERSE ONE HUNDRED FIFTY-EIGHT</u>: *"I beheld the transgressors, and was grieved; because they kept not thy word."*

When I view people who are living ungodly, mistreating their families, etc., it grieves my spirit; it not only grieves me, it causes me to want to shake them and sometimes it angers me! Particularly when there are innocent children involved. I have to be honest, if my spirit was in control, I would really mess up the situation.

We must give way the leading of the Holy Ghost to do the right thing.

"Finally, my brethren, be strong in the Lord, and in the power of his might. Put on the whole armour of God, that ye may be able to stand against the wiles of the devil. For we wrestle not against flesh and blood, but against principalities, against powers, against the rulers of the darkness of this world, against spiritual wickedness in high places. Wherefore take unto you the whole armour of God, that ye may be able to withstand in the evil day, and having done all, to stand. Stand therefore, having your loins girt about with truth, and having on the breastplate of righteousness; And your feet shod with the preparation of the gospel of peace; Above all, taking the shield of faith, wherewith ye shall be able to quench all the fiery darts of the wicked. And take the helmet of salvation, and the sword of the Spirit, which is the word of God: Praying always with all prayer and supplication in the Spirit, and watching thereunto with all perseverance and supplication for all saints." Ephesians 6: 10-18

<u>*VERSE ONE HUNDRED FIFTY-NINE:*</u> *"Consider how I love thy precepts: quicken me, O LORD, according to thy lovingkindness."*

I have always loved the Lord and had a great respect for the Bible, but as I have grown older, I have a greater regard for the Word. It has become my safe harbor. When I am sad, it makes me glad; when I feel left out, it makes me feel special; when I am hungry [not for food], it feeds me; when I am angry, it calms me down; when I need a close friend, Jesus is near me; when I need rest, he the Word settles me; and when I don't feel well physically. he gently heals me of my malady. The Trinity is my all in all. He loves me enough to know me and scold me if necessary! God is not only my creator; he is my Abba Father with whom I love to fellowship.

I am not like John. I have never seen Jesus or my Father, but I feel the Trinity very close to me, as they live in and dwell within me.

> *"That which was from the beginning, which we have heard, which we have seen with our eyes, which we have looked upon, and our hands have handled, of the Word of life; (For the life was manifested, and we have seen it, and bear witness, and shew unto you that eternal life, which was with the Father, and was manifested unto us;) That which we have seen and heard declare we unto you, that ye also may have fellowship with us: and truly our fellowship is with the Father, and with his Son Jesus Christ. And these things write we unto you, that your joy may be full. This then is the message which we have heard of him, and declare unto you, that God is light, and in him is no darkness at all. If we say that we have fellowship with him, and walk in darkness, we lie, and do not the truth: But if we walk in the light, as he is in the light, we have fellowship one with another, and the blood of Jesus Christ his Son cleanseth us from all sin." 1 John 1: 1-7*

> <u>*VERSE ONE HUNDRED SIXTY:*</u> *"Thy word is true from the beginning: and every one of thy righteous judgments endureth forever."*

Those who are truly born again by the Spirit know the Word is truth because they have walked in the Word and it has never led astray. It is a true and faithful guide. I am a dyed-in-the-wool King James Bible believer. I know humans translated the King James Bible, but I believe they were dedicated, educated Christians who loved God and followed the leading of the Holy Ghost in the process of translating from the Hebrew and Greek.

I do not judge people who use new translations; however, there are some that have deleted the blood from the Holy Script. Such translations are liars and far from the truth.

The King James Bible has stood the test since the mid 1600s and that's good enough for me.

> *"In the beginning was the Word, and the Word was with God, and the Word was God. The same was in the beginning with God. All things were made by him; and without him was not anything made that was made. In him was life; and the life was the light of men. And the light shineth in darkness; and the darkness comprehended it not. There was a man sent from God whose name was John. The same came for a witness, to bear witness of the Light, that all men through him might believe. He was not that Light, but was sent to bear witness of that Light. That was the true Light, which lighteth every man that cometh into the world. He was in the world, and the world was made by him, and the world knew him not. He came unto his own, and his own received him not. But as many as received him, to them gave he power to become the sons of God, even to them that believe on his name: Which were born, not of blood, nor of the will of the flesh, nor of the will of man, but of God. And the Word was made flesh, and dwelt among us, and we be witness of him, and cried, saying, This was he of whom I spake, He that cometh after me is preferred before me: for he was before me." John 1: 1-15*

UNIT TWENTY-ONE:
SCHIN
Psalm 119: 161-168

VERSE ONE HUNDRED SIXTY-ONE: *"Princes have perse-cuted me without a cause: but my heart standeth in awe of thy word."*

As I stated previously, I study the WORD in the present tense, not for historical reasoning. History is important; however, we need to know how the Word affects our daily life in the 21st century.

When I read this Scripture, I think how our government is changing to meet the needs of the culture of human beings. However, I have made up my mind that I will stand on the Word and reverence my God instead of bending to the culture and the laws that have changed to include various sinful activities. Taxing sin is not eliminating the problems of sinful activities!

Shadrack, Meshach, and Abednego did not bow to the image Nebuchadnezzar made and were thrown into the furnace and the Lord was with them. They were not burned and did not have the smell of smoke upon them because they trusted God. They stood firm and stated:

"…we are not careful to answer thee in this matter. If it be so, our God whom we serve is able to deliver us from the burning fiery furnace, and he will deliver us out of thine hand, O king. But if not, be it known unto thee, O king, that we will not serve thy gods,

Daniel, when he knew the conspiracy was formed against him, continued worshipping God openly three times a day. He was thrown into the lion's den, and they did not harm him. Read Daniel 6 for the whole story.

You and I may face some terrible problems in the future of our country, but let us not be afraid and build up our most Holy Faith against that day.

"Jude, the servant of Jesus Christ, and brother of James, to them that are sanctified by God the Father, and preserved in Jesus Christ, and called: and peace, and love, be multiplied. Beloved, when I gave all diligence to write unto you of the common salvation, it was needful for me to write unto you, and exhort you that ye should earnestly contend for the faith which was once delivered unto the saints. For there are certain men crept in unawares, who were before of old ordained to this condemnation, ungodly men, turning the grace of our God into lasciviousness, and denying the only Lord God, and our Lord Jesus Christ. I will therefore put you in remembrance, though ye once knew this, how that the Lord, having saved the people out of the land of Egypt, afterward destroyed them that believed not. And the angels which kept not their first estate, but left their own habitation, he hath reserved in everlasting chains under darkness unto the judgment of the great day. Even as Sodom and Gomorrha, and the cities about them in like manner, giving themselves over to fornication, and going after strange flesh, are set forth for an example, suffering the vengeance of eternal fire. Likewise also these filthy dreamers defile the flesh, despise dominion, and speak evil of dignities. Yet Michael the archangel, when contending with the devil he disputed about the body of Moses, durst not bring against him a railing accusation, but said, The Lord rebuke thee. But these speak evil of those things which they know not: but what they know naturally, as brute beasts, in those things they corrupt themselves. Woe unto them! for they have gone in the way of Cain, and ran greedily after the error of Balaam for reward, and perished in the gainsaying of Core. These are spots in your feasts of charity, when they feast with you, feeding themselves without fear: clouds they are without water, carried about of winds; trees whose fruit withereth, without fruit, twice dead, plucked up by the roots; Raging waves of the sea, foaming out their own shame; wan-

*dering stars, to whom is reserved the blackness of darkness forever.
And Enoch also, the seventh from Adam, prophesied of these, saying, Behold, the Lord cometh with ten thousandof his saints, To ex-
ecute judgment upon all, and to convince all that are ungodly
among them of all their ungodly deeds which they have ungodly
committed, and of all their hard speeches which ungodly sinners
have spoken against him. These are murmurers, complainers,
walking after their own lusts; and their mouth speaketh great
swelling words, having men's persons in admiration because of ad-
vantage. But, beloved, remember ye the words which were spoken
before of the apostles of our Lord Jesus Christ; How that they told
you there should be mockers in the last time, who should walk after
their own ungodly lusts. These be they who separate themselves,
sensual, having not the Spirit. But ye, beloved, building up yourselves on your most holy faith, praying in the Holy Ghost, Keep
yourselves in the love of God, looking for the mercy of our Lord
Jesus Christ unto eternal life. And of some have compassion, making a difference: And others save with fear, pulling them out of the
fire; hating even the garment spotted by the flesh. Now unto him
that is able to keep you from falling, and to present you faultless
before the presence of his glory with exceeding joy, To the only wise
God our Saviour, be glory and majesty, dominion and power, both
now and ever. Amen." The Book of Jude*

*VERSE ONE HUNDRED SIXTY-TWO: "I rejoice at thy word,
as one that findeth great spoil."*

When I look back at my life, I rejoice for the many times the Word of
God was proven to be true and my safe haven of rest. There were times when
it seemed that all was lost physically, spiritually and financially. But at the end
of every trial when I would lay all on the altar before the Lord, he would always
be there for me. You see, all the popularity, self-assertion and financial goals I
was seeking became fulfilled in my relationship with my heavenly Father
through the Lord Jesus Christ. He is my greatest and most dependable asset
I have. He is my all in all, my true God!

*"I will extol thee, O LORD; for thou hast lifted me up, and hast
not made my foes to rejoice over me. O LORD my God, I cried
unto thee, and thou hast healed me. O LORD, thou hast brought*

up my soul from the grave: thou hast kept me alive, that I should not go down to the pit. Sing unto the LORD, O ye saints of his, and give thanks at the remembrance of his holiness. For his anger endureth but a moment; in his favour is life: weeping may endure for a night, but joy cometh in the morning. And in my prosperity I said, I shall never be moved. LORD, by thy favour thou hast made my mountain to stand strong: thou didst hide thy face, and I was troubled. I cried to thee, O LORD; and unto the LORD I made supplication. What profit is there in my blood, when I go down to the pit? Shall the dust praise thee? shall it declare thy truth? Hear, O LORD, and have mercy upon me: LORD, be thou my helper. Thou hast turned for me my mourning into dancing: thou hast put off my sackcloth, and girded me with gladness; To the end that my glory may sing praise to thee, and not be silent. O LORD my God, I will give thanks unto thee for ever." Psalm 30: 1-12

<u>VERSE ONE HUNDRED SIXTY-THREE:</u> *"I hate and abhor lying: but thy law do I love."*

When life is based upon a lie, it will not profit a person. One lie leads to another lie to verify the first, second or third. When the truth is finally found out, it is harder to regain one's confidence. It is best to always be truthful because there is less pain and trouble to work through to regain one's trust!

The Word is truth; may we keep close to the truth and be not deceived or try to deceive another. The wicked lie to deceive to profit themselves! They always lose !

"The wicked in his pride doth persecute the poor: let them be taken in the devices that they have imagined. For the wicked boasteth of his heart's desire, and blesseth the covetous, whom the LORD abhorreth. The wicked, through the pride of his countenance, will not seek after God: God is not in all his thoughts. His ways are always grievous; thy judgments are far above out of his sight: as for all his enemies, he puffeth at them. He hath said in his heart, I shall not be moved: for I shall never be in adversity. His mouth is full of cursing and deceit and fraud: under his tongue is mischief and vanity. He sitteth in the lurking places of the villages: in the secret places doth he murder the innocent: his eyes are privily set against

the poor. He lieth in wait secretly as a lion in his den: he lieth in wait to catch the poor: he doth catch the poor, when he draweth him into his net. He croucheth, and humbleth himself, that the poor may fall by his strong ones. He hath said in his heart, God hath forgotten: he hideth his face; he will never see it. Arise, O LORD; O God, lift up thine hand: forget not the humble. Wherefore doth the wicked contemn God? he hath said in his heart, Thou wilt not require it. Thou hast seen it; for thou beholdest mischief and spite, to requite it with thy hand: the poor committeth himself unto thee; thou art the helper of the fatherless. Break thou the arm of the wicked and the evil man: seek out his wickedness till thou find none. The LORD is King for ever and ever: the heathen are perished out of his land. LORD, thou hast heard the desire of the humble: thou wilt prepare their heart, thou wilt cause thine ear to hear:" Psalm 10: 2-17

<u>*VERSE ONE HUNDRED SIXTY-FOUR:*</u> *"Seven times a day do I praise thee because of thy righteous judgments."*

I have learned it is always proper to praise the Lord, even when things are not going my way. Why? Because when things are going my way, they are usually going the wrong way. When we praise the Lord, he hears us, even when it is sacrificial. He knows we are trying to do the right thing despite the craving of the flesh.

Praising the Lord increases right judgments because words of exaltation increase the presence of the Holy Ghost in our spirit who not only leads into all truth but victory as well. Think about it; happy thoughts increase joy in our spirit!

Seven is the perfect number, but let's not limit happiness; the Lord does many things throughout the day to deserve our praise! Praise increases our devotion and fidelity to our Father!

<u>*VERSE ONE HUNDRED SIXTY-FIVE:*</u> *"Great peace, have they which love thy law: and nothing shall offend them."*

When we think on the Word of God and crave to learn more of it, we have great calmness of mind. We are not troubled and anxious. We believe and feel that all things are well-ordered by God and have the assurance of the best results. So we calmly leave all the future to him. The love of God's Word is the best; in fact, it is the only way to secure permanent peace in the soul.

Being in the ministry, especially the pastoral ministry, this verse is one the most important and powerful verses a minster must memorize! It will help one overcome any and every fowl word or rumor uttered against you. This verse helps us in our homes also *if* we will practice using it and watching our body language and words. Unfortunately, being together with our spouse or children, we sometimes utter the wrong words and react instead of acting on the promise of this verse.

> *"For he that will love life, and see good days, let him refrain his tongue from evil, and his lips that they speak no guile: Let him eschew evil, and do good; let him seek peace, and ensue it. For the eyes of the Lord are over the righteous, and his ears are open unto their prayers: but the face of the Lord is against them that do evil. And who is he that will harm you, if ye be followers of that which is good? But and if ye suffer for righteousness' sake, happy are ye: and be not afraid of their terror, neither be troubled; But sanctify the Lord God in your hearts: and be ready always to give an answer to every man that asketh you a reason of the hope that is in you with meekness and fear: Having a good conscience; that, whereas they speak evil of you, as of evildoers, they may be ashamed that falsely accuse your good conversation in Christ. For it is better, if the will of God be so, that ye suffer for well doing, than for evil doing." 1 Peter 3: 10-17*

> <u>*VERSE ONE HUNDRED SIXTY-SIX:*</u> *"LORD, I have hoped for thy salvation, and done thy commandments."*

Hope for my salvation is an ongoing desire in my life. In fact, I am looking forward to seeing Jesus one of these days either in death or the rapture. That event is constantly on my mind. Therefore, I constantly strive to keep the Word and God's commandments in the forefront of my thinking.

> *"Therefore being justified by faith, we have peace with God through our Lord Jesus Christ: By whom also we have access by faith into this grace wherein we stand, and rejoice in hope of the glory of God. And not only so, but we glory in tribulations also: knowing that*

tribulation worketh patience; And patience, experience; and experience, hope: And hope maketh not ashamed; because the love of God is shed abroad in our hearts by the Holy Ghost which is given unto us. For when we were yet without strength, in due time Christ died for the ungodly. For scarcely for a righteous man will one die: yet peradventure for a good man some would even dare to die. But God commendeth his love toward us, in that, while we were yet sinners, Christ died for us. Much more then, being now justified by his blood, we shall be saved from wrath through him." Romans 5: 1-9

<u>*VERSE ONE HUNDRED SIXTY-SEVEN*</u>*: "My soul hath kept thy testimonies; and I love them exceedingly."*

I thank Jesus for praying the Father to send the Holy Ghost to me, particularly the Baptism of the Holy Ghost. For it is through the power of the Holy Ghost I am learning more of the Word of God which enables me to live a life of an overcomer. He also helps me when I have the tendency to be tempted with the things of this world instead of keeping my self-focused on my eternal goal. My love for the Word of God is increased as the Holy Ghost guides me daily.

"Ask, and it shall be given you; seek, and ye shall find; knock, and it shall be opened unto you: For every one that asketh receiveth; and he that seeketh findeth; and to him that knocketh it shall be opened. Or what man is there of you, whom if his son ask bread, will he give him a stone? Or if he ask a fish, will he give him a serpent? If ye then, being evil, know how to give good gifts unto your children, how much more shall your Father which is in heaven give good things to them that ask him? Therefore all things whatsoever ye would that men should do to you, do ye even so to them: for this is the law and the prophets. Enter ye in at the strait gate: for wide is the gate, and broad is the way, that leadeth to destruction, and many there be which go in there at: Because strait is the gate, and narrow is the way, which leadeth unto life, and few there be that find it." Matthew 7: 7-14

"And I say unto you, Ask, and it shall be given you; seek, and ye shall find; knock, and it shall be opened unto you. For every one that asketh receiveth; and he that seeketh findeth; and to him that

knocketh it shall be opened. If a son shall ask bread of any of you that is a father, will he give him a stone? or if he ask a fish, will he for a fish give him a serpent? Or if he shall ask an egg, will he offer him a scorpion? If ye then, being evil, know how to give good gifts unto your children: how much more shall your heavenly Father give the Holy Spirit to them that ask him?" Luke 11: 9-13

<u>*VERSE ONE HUNDRED SIXTY-EIGHT*</u>*: "I have kept thy precepts and thy testimonies: for all my ways are before thee."*

All my ways are before the Lord; he is not pleased if I serve him in self-righteousness. He is my righteousness, and it is my dependence on the precious Holy Ghost that helps me keep his Word and walk accordingly.

I am weak, but he is strong; I am unlearned, but he is my truth and confidence. His word is truth!

"Unto thee, O LORD, do I lift up my soul. O my God, I trust in thee: let me not be ashamed, let not mine enemies triumph over me.Yea, let none that wait on thee be ashamed: let them be ashamed which transgress without cause. Shew me thy ways, O LORD; teach me thy paths. Lead me in thy truth, and teach me: for thou art the God of my salvation; on thee do I wait all the day. Remember, O LORD, thy tender mercies and thy lovingkindnesses; for they have been ever of old. Remember not the sins of my youth, nor my transgressions: according to thy mercy remember thou me for thy goodness' sake, O LORD. Good and upright is the LORD: therefore will he teach sinners in the way. The meek will he guide in judgment: and the meek will he teach his way. All the paths of the LORD are mercy and truth unto such as keep his covenant and his testimonies. For thy name's sake, O LORD, pardon mine iniquity; for it is great. What man is he that feareth the LORD? him shall he teach in the way that he shall choose. His soul shall dwell at ease; and his seed shall inherit the earth. The secret of the LORD is with them that fear him; and he will shew them his covenant." Psalm 25: 1-14

UNIT TWENTY-TWO:

TAU
Psalm 119: 169-176

<u>*VERSE ONE HUNDRED SIXTY-NINE:*</u> *"Let my cry come near before thee, O LORD: give me understanding according to thy word."*

In the Old Testament times, there was not an intercessor for mankind as we have in the New Testament. Now we have an intercessor—his name is Jesus the Christ—who knows how difficult our journey is. I thank God for the Holy Ghost who is leading me, but I am praying for more understanding and wisdom to live out the rest of my life.

The wise words the apostle Paul gave Timothy is the challenge for we who are in ministry the 21st century.

> *"Thou therefore endure hardness, as a good soldier of Jesus Christ. No man that warreth entangleth himself with the affairs of this life; that he may please him who hath chosen him to be a soldier. And if a man also strive for masteries, yet is he not crowned, except he strive lawfully. The husbandman that laboureth must be first partaker of the fruits. Consider what I say; and the Lord give thee understanding in all things. Remember that Jesus Christ of the seed of David was raised from the dead according to my gospel." 2 Timothy 2: 3-8*

<u>*VERSE ONE HUNDRED SEVENTY:*</u> *"Let my supplication come before thee: deliver me according to thy word."*

When I find myself in a position of stress, my prayer becomes more serious than at other times. Even though I know that trials come to all to strengthen our faith, there are times that I desire that they be shortened. Of course I believe all born again by the Spirit believers want the will of the Lord, so I humbly ask for deliverance as quickly as possible. I believe the Lord is moved by our attitude instead of our request.

"For thus saith the high and lofty One that inhabiteth eternity, whose name is Holy; I dwell in the high and holy place, with him also that is of a contrite and humble spirit, to revive the spirit of the humble, and to revive the heart of the contrite ones. For I will not contend for ever, neither will I be always wroth: for the spirit should fail before me, and the souls which I have made." Isaiah 57: 15, 16

VERSE ONE HUNDRED SEVENTY-ONE: "My lips shall utter praise, when thou hast taught me thy statutes."

When we are more concerned about learning his Word, it lessens our desire to complain or grumble about life's troubles that come now and then. We must always remember that serving the Lord is a privilege of fellowship as well as a command.

"Give unto the LORD the glory due unto his name; worship the LORD in the beauty of holiness. The voice of the LORD is upon the waters: the God of glory thundereth: the LORD is upon many waters. The voice of he LORD is powerful; the voice of the LORD is full of majesty." Psalm 29: 2-4

"Oh how great is thy goodness, which thou hast laid up for them that fear thee; which thou hast wrought for them that trust in thee before the sons of men! Thou shalt hide them in the secret of thy presence from the pride of man: thou shalt keep them secretly in a pavilion from the strife of tongues." Psalm 31: 19, 20

VERSE ONE HUNDRED SEVENTY-TWO: "My tongue shall speak of thy word: for all thy commandments are righteousness."

It is my prayer that the Holy Ghost will help me order my conversation in order not to spread gossip or sow seeds of discord among the church. Let all my words be represented of your righteousness, not self-righteousness.

"Let your conversation be without covetousness; and be content with such things as ye have: for he hath said, I will never leave thee, nor forsake thee. So that we may boldly say, The Lord is my helper, and I will not fear what man shall do unto me. Remember them which have the rule over you, who have spoken unto you the word of God: whose faith follow, considering the end of their conversation." Hebrews 13: 5-7

VERSE ONE HUNDRED SEVENTY-THREE: "Let thine hand help me; for I have chosen thy precepts."

I love the old hymn "Hand in Hand with Jesus" written by Johnson Outman, Jr. and l. D. Huffstutler in 1940. I have read and sung it many times during my lifetime, even before I became a born again by the Spirit Christian.

VERSE ONE:

Once from my poor sin-sick soul Christ did ev'ry burden roll,
Now I walk redeemed and whole, hand in hand with Jesus.

VERSE TWO;

In my night of dark despair, Jesus heard and answered pray'r,
Now I'm walking free as air, hand in hand with Jesus.

VERSE THREE;

From the straight and narrow way, paise the Lord,
I cannot stray, for I'm walking ev'ry day, hand in hand with Jesus.

VERSE FOUR;

When the stars are backward rolled and his home I shall behold,
I will walk those streets of gold, hand in hand with Jesus.

CHORUS:

Hand in hand we walk each day, hand in hand along the way,
walking thus, I cannot stray, hand in hand with Jesus.

Note: "Hand in Hand with Jesus" authored by Rev. John Oatman Jr. and I. D Huffstutder; copyright by Stamps Baxter music BMI; all rights controlled by The Benson Company Inc. Nashville, TN.

"This then is the message which we have heard of him, and declare unto you, that God is light, and in him is no darkness at all. If we say that we have fellowship with him, and walk in darkness, we lie, and do not the truth: But if we walk in the light, as he is in the light, we have fellowship one with another, and the blood of Jesus Christ his Son cleanseth us from all sin." 1 John 1: 5-7

<u>VERSE ONE HUNDRED SEVENTY-FOUR</u>: "I have longed for thy salvation, O LORD; and thy law is my delight."

Jesus is the Word, and I delighted to read and study it upon this earth, but my greatest desire is to see the one who made it possible for me to become a born again by the Spirit Christian.

"John answered them, saying, I baptize with water: but there standeth one among you, whom ye know not; He it is, who coming after me is preferred before me, whose shoe's latchet I am not worthy to unloose. these things were done in Bethabara beyond Jordan, where John was baptizing. The next day John seeth Jesus coming unto him, and saith, Behold the Lamb of God, which taketh away the sin of the world. This is he of whom I said, After me cometh a man which is preferred before me: for he was before me. And I knew him not: but that he should be made manifest to Israel, therefore am I come baptizing with water. And John bare record, saying, I saw the Spirit descending from heaven like a dove, and it abode upon him. And I knew him not: but he that sent me to baptize with water, the same said unto me, Upon whom thou shalt see the Spirit descending, and remaining on him, the same is he which baptizeth with the Holy Ghost. And I saw, and bare record that this is the Son of God. Again the next day after John stood, and two of his disciples; And looking upon Jesus as he walked, he saith, Behold the Lamb of God!" John 1: 26-36

One day, our mortal bodies, whether in the grave or alive *<u>in Christ,</u>* will raise and be changed in the twinkling of an eye and we shall behold him face to face. Hallelujah! I Corinthians 15: 52-58; 1 Thessalonians 4: 13-18

VERSE ONE HUNDRED SEVENTY-FIVE: *"Let my soul live, and it shall praise thee; and let thy judgments help me."*

Have you ever heard someone say *"they really lived"* about someone who has just passed away? They usually are referring to how a person succeeded in life, how much partying they did, etc. in the worldly sense, but when they say that about a Christian when they pass, they usually mean how faithful they were to Christ and how many souls they won to the Lord during their lifetime.

"I beseech you therefore, brethren, by the mercies of God, that ye present your bodies a living sacrifice, holy, acceptable unto God, which is your reasonable service. And be not conformed to this world: but be ye transformed by the renewing of your mind, that ye may prove what is that good, and acceptable, and perfect, will of God." Romans 12: 1-2

VERSE ONE HUNDRED SEVENTY-SIX: *"I have gone astray like a lost sheep; seek thy servant; for I do not forget thy commandments."*

Everyone has gone astray at one time or another. Even born again by the Spirit Christians have a tendency to wander when they do not faithfully read and study the Word. The attractions of this world are many, and everyone is distracted; if they say they have not been, they lie.

The parable of the lost sheep in Luke 15: 4-7 is a prime example of how important one person is to God, especially one of the household of faith. The Shepherd leaves the 99 and goes in search of the one sheep because he loves that sheep, and when he finds it, he brings it home and rejoices with his friends!

"For the Son of man is come to seek and to save that which was lost." Luke 19: 10

"Herein is my Father glorified, that ye bear much fruit; so shall ye be my disciples. As the Father hath loved me, so have I loved you: continue ye in my love. If ye keep my commandments, ye shall abide in my love; even as I have kept my Father's commandments, and abide in his love. These things have I spoken unto you, that my joy

might remain in you, and that your joy might be full. This is my commandment, That ye love one another, as I have loved you. Greater love hath no man than this, that a man lay down his life for his friends. Ye are my friends, if ye do whatsoever I command you." John 15: 8-14

As I close Reflections of Psalm 119, it is my hope and prayer whoever happens to find it will read it and meditate upon some of the experiences and the special Scriptures I have worked through and studied in my life and will find what they need to live a victorious overcoming life.

It is my desire to see many come to the full knowledge of God's love and concern for each person that seriously studies the Word of the LIVING GOD. Each Word in the Bible, even the disciplinary portions are filled with SPIRIT AND LIFE!

At this moment, I am 81 years of age; the Holy Ghost started dealing with me when I was turned 79 to start writing this study. My prayer for each person who reads *The Personal Reflections of Psalm 119* is that the Holy Ghost will begin to work in their personal life and show them THE LIGHT which is JESUS that will guide you into greater victory!

May God Richly Bless and Keep You!
Kenneth O. Light
Research materials used:
The King James Bible;
Strong's Exhaustive Concordance of the Bible;
Webster's New Twentieth Century Dictionary;
Spurgeon's writings; Kenneth Hagan's writings;
years of ministry as a missionary, evangelist and pastor;
Matthew Henry's Commentary on the Whole Bible,
and various Biblesoft, Inc. Copyright 1997, 2003, 2005, 2006
Electronic Database references.

ABOUT THE AUTHOR:
Kenneth O. Light

Marriage, child-rearing becoming socially and financially successful were the top four priorities in his life until 1967; then he met Christ and everything in his life changed drastically. He was baptized in water and received the gift of the Baptism in the Holy Ghost soon after.

He and his wife entered service in his vineyard in New Mexico/Arizona as lay *(self-supported)* missionaries in 1968. In 1974, they began their ministry as evangelists, singing and operating in the Gifts of the Spirit. Ken received his Exhorters License and License to Preach in 1975; then he studied through the Berean School of the Bible for ten years and was ordained by The Assemblies of God in 1991; was bi-vocational until 1996 while serving churches as interim, associate and full-time pastorates. In 1996, he retired from corporate work and served as Senior Pastor in three churches. He is now retired and fills pulpits as needed at the time.

Cloe has served in many capacities with her husband: pianist for all the churches pastored, music ministry, Sunday school teacher, Bible seminar teacher, youth leader, women's minister leader, etc.

Now at the age of 81, he is spending more time with his wife and family. He is looking for and loving the coming of Jesus very soon.

Ken and his wife Cloe reside in Cherokee Village, Arkansas. They have two sons and four grandchildren.